Residential Property Acquisition Handbook

By
John T. Reed

John T. Reed
342 Bryan Drive
Danville, CA 94526
415-820-6292

To Arthur W. Tunnell, Jr.,
my father-in-law,
who told me ten years ago
to write this book.

Copyright January 1991 John T. Reed
Third printing: May 1991

Published by John T. Reed
342 Bryan Drive
Danville, CA 94526
415-820-6292

Manufactured in the United States of America
by Cal-West Printing & Graphics, Concord, Ca.
Library of Congress Catalog Card Number: 90-091781
ISBN: 0-939224-22-4

OTHER MATERIAL BY JOHN T. REED

- *Aggressive Tax Avoidance for Real Estate Investors* (book)
- *Distressed Real Estate Times: Offensive and Defensive Strategy and Tactics Special Report* (cassettes or book)
- *High Leverage Real Estate Finance* (cassettes)
- *How to Buy Real Estate for at Least 20% Below Market Value, Vol. I and II* (cassettes)
- *How to Find Deals that Make Sense in Today's Market* (cassettes)
- *How to Increase the Value of Real Estate* (book)
- *How to Manage Residential Property for Maximum Cash Flow and Resale Value* (cassettes or book)
- *How to Save Tens of Thousands of Tax Dollars by Exchanging* (cassettes)
- *How to Use Leverage to Maximize Your Real Estate Investment Return* (book)
- *John T. Reed's Real Estate Investor's Monthly* (newsletter)
- *Single-Family Lease Options Special Report* (cassettes or book)
- *Office Building Acquisition Handbook*
- *Real Estate Investor's Monthly on Real Estate Investment Strategy* (book)

For more information, see the order forms in the front and back of this book or contact John T. Reed, 342 Bryan Drive, Danville, CA 94526, or call 800-635-5425.

THANKS TO...

Gil Kemp for publishing my first book...my wife, Marty Tunnell for designing and producing this one...Mike Scott for his willingness to share his knowledge of the apartment brokerage business.

ABOUT THE AUTHOR

John T. Reed is a real estate writer and investor.

His real estate work experience includes home, land, and investment property brokerage and residential and nonresidential property management. As a property manager, he managed apartment complexes, office buildings, industrial space, farms, and single-family rental houses.

He has invested in New Jersey, Texas, and California.

He is the editor and publisher of *John T. Reed's Real Estate Investor's Monthly*, a national newsletter...and the author and publisher of seven books on various real estate investment subjects.

Mr. Reed has been interviewed about real estate by Morley Safer on *60 Minutes*, by David Hartman on *Good Morning America*, and by Larry King on *Larry King Live* as well as other television and radio programs. His analysis of real estate investing has appeared in *The Wall Street Journal*, *Newsweek*, *U.S. News & World Report*, *Changing Times*, *Money*, and various real estate journals.

He holds a Bachelor of Science degree from West Point and a Master of Business Administration degree from Harvard Business School.

Residential Property Acquisition Handbook

CONTENTS

PREFACE

When I began real estate investing, I looked for a book of check lists like this one. But I couldn't find one. So I made mistakes. In my work as a real estate salesman and as a member of real estate investment clubs, I also watched other people make mistakes. Then, I made lists of those mistakes to make sure I wouldn't make them again. From those mistake lists I made check lists, and from the check lists came this book.

If you are considering buying a home or investing in a rental house or apartment building, this book could save you a great deal of time, money, effort, and emotional strain. Use this book to prepare for your inspections and negotiations. Carry it with you when you inspect the property. Use it as a guide when you are reconstructing an income and expense statement, drafting a contract, etc.

If you only read this book and add it to your investment library, you have missed its main point. You can't learn what is in this book any more than an airline pilot can learn his preflight check list. In the acquisition of a house or apartment building, accuracy and thoroughness are essential, and it is too easy for even a veteran investor...or pilot...to forget one of the many important steps. Real estate investing does not have the life or death aspects of flying a plane, but the stakes are still high. And those high stakes demand the high standards of accuracy and thoroughness that are attainable only through the use of written check lists.

Keep in mind that there are two memory problems in buying residential property: You must remember both what to look at and what you saw when you looked. This book will tell you what to look at. But you'll need a pencil and paper and camera to remember what you saw. So TAKE THE BOOK and TAKE NOTES and TAKE PICTURES.

A caveat

Buying real estate, like politics, is the art of the possible. A successful investor is one who achieves a worthwhile return on his investment. Care and thoroughness in property selection are important to investment success, but they are not ends in themselves. Too often, people are convinced by textbooks and case histories that they should invest in real estate...but they are paralyzed when the time comes to actually sign on the dotted line. Used improperly, this book might contribute to that sort of "analysis paralysis."

If you decide you shouldn't buy a property unless it meets all the "tests" in this book, you'll never invest. The perfect property doesn't exist. Indeed, properties with problems usually offer more opportunity for profit. This book's purpose is to help you assess problems accurately, not avoid them entirely.

Some readers may think that the scope of this book is a model for the thoroughness of each acquisition evaluation you make. That would be ideal, but an investment never takes place in a vacuum. There will nearly always be other potential investors looking at a property at the same time you are. If they consistently reach agreements with the owner while you are still on page 8, you'll never be an investor.

You have to keep one eye on the check lists and the other on the deal. It's a fact of life that we rarely have "enough" information when a decision has to be made. To be a successful investor, you must make **timely** offers. And your price must be high enough to be acceptable to the seller.

One good way to make sure you not only analyze properties but also take action is to set a **deadline** for buying a property. Six months is probably sufficient time to find a suitable investment. If you've been looking longer than that and haven't found an "acceptable" property, you're probably:

(1) Being too fussy,
(2) Taking too long to evaluate each property, or
(3) Making unrealistic offers.

Establish a standard for the amount of time you take between when you learn a property is available and when you make a decision about bidding on it. This should be **short**, maybe two business days.

Try to complete as many of the check lists as possible during that period. If you are certain that you don't have enough information by the end of that time, advise the owner of your continued interest and give him the date you expect to make a decision. If he insists on an earlier decision, either because he has another offer or because he wants to give you the bum's rush, say goodbye and look at other properties. But keep the six-month rule in mind. If you continually turn down investment opportunities because of too little time, you're probably too slow.

One way to make a speedier evaluation is to recruit a team from members of your family, friends, or fellow investors. Assign each team member a different part of the check lists, a different room of the house or apartment to inspect, or different places to call for expense verification.

If your team is properly prepared and led, you can complete virtually all of the check lists within two days. Of course, completion of **every** item on **every** check list is not necessary. The main dangers are toxic contamination, bad location, and a structure which cannot be economically repaired in view of the price, terms, and cash available. Most other problems are cheaply correctable. If you feel pressed to make a decision on a property and you're convinced the location is good and the property is clean and the structure is sound, you should probably go ahead even though you are uncertain about other less important items.

In his book *Games People Play*, Eric Berne described one adult behavior pattern that he called "Now I've Got You, You Son of a Bitch." This refers to the enjoyment we derive from catching someone in an act of dishonesty. Selling a large building is a situation in which people are tempted to conceal or minimize problems and exaggerate net income.

This book provides you with the tools to uncover most deceptions and exaggerations and to confront the seller with evidence of his dishonesty. Restrain yourself. It is important to retain the seller's goodwill throughout the negotiations. In some cases, subtle references to apparent discrepancies can play on a seller's guilt feelings and may help you gain a negotiating advantage. But be careful not to overdo it.

This book is not intended to be a complete text on houses or apartments. It is simply a book of check lists and, as such, contains only those things which are "checklistable." To be successful in real estate investing, you need a broader education than this book provides. If your are buying a rental property, you should also join the local apartment owners association before you begin your search in an area. If there is no local association, start one.

John T. Reed
Danville, California

HOW TO USE THIS BOOK

Residential buildings are complex properties. Even a small building contains hundreds of feet of plumbing pipes, dozens of plumbing fixtures, hundreds of yards of wiring, thousands of square yards of carpet, complicated heating systems, and so forth. Many properties contain substances or problems now considered to be dangerous contaminants like asbestos and leaking underground storage tanks.

Rental income is sometimes dependent upon multiple leases that often contain a variety of terms. Expenses include dozens of items that must be verified or accurately estimated. Detailed purchase and mortgage contracts must be signed, and everything must be completed at closing, often in a closing meeting attended by representatives of lenders, title insurers, and the parties to the agreement of sale. Clearly, this is a process in which check lists are necessary - for the expert as well as the novice.

Residential Property Acquisition Handbook is meant to be **used** not just **read**. Space is left for you to check off items as you see them and to write down your notes.

Your notes in this book will provide a written record to help you evaluate potential investments. If you'll be evaluating many properties, I suggest you buy multiple copies of this book. There is also additional space at the end of each section and at the end of the book for you to use as you'd like. You may wish to make general observations, summarize a property's good points and problems, or jog your memory with simple plans of rooms or sketches of problem areas.

Houses versus apartment buildings

My first book was called *Apartment Investing Check Lists*. It was written strictly for people who buy apartment buildings. But several people, including my father-in-law, noted that it would be equally useful for a home buyer. So I have written this book to be used by both home buyers and investors who buy multi-million dollar apartment complexes.

Big-time apartment investors often sniff at those who buy houses, condos, and duplexes as small time. And some of them may disdain this book because it's aimed at home buyers in part. Not big time enough.

Home buyers, on the other hand, may feel they are wasting money on stuff not aimed at them like discussions of residents. That's true for a small percentage of the information in this book. But much of the information which appears to be investor related only is also useful for home buyers.

Investors are, in a sense, nothing but extremely careful real estate buyers. Most home buyers ought to be more careful than they are. So home buyers would benefit from reading and using most of the seemingly investment-oriented material in this book. For example, home owners rarely use the term HVAC (heating, ventilating, and air-conditioning). But they usually have both heating and air-conditioning in their home. And they often have ventilating equipment like attic fans. So it would be a good idea for home buyers to check with an HVAC guy before they buy.

The main reason I combined both home and apartment building material in the same book is that the alternative would be to publish two separate books. Then, there would be considerable overlap between the two books and I would no doubt get complaints from readers who did not appreciate paying twice for the same information.

So if you are a big-time apartment complex investor, congratulations on your success. I know you'll find this book valuable if not invaluable. I hope you won't mind my occasionally addressing the home buyers who are using this book.

And if you are a single-family home buyer, you too will probably find the book invaluable. I urge you not to tune out when I seem to be addressing the investor reader. You can learn a lot that may help you by paying attention to those passages.

PART ONE: INVESTMENT STRATEGY

1

Residential Property Investment Strategy

Who needs income?

Until the seventies, residential buildings were a rather mundane investment…like stock in the electric company or some such. But in the seventies, a couple new factors were "invented" that dramatically changed residential investing:

- Inflation.
- Rent control.

Inflation raised building values by raising the rents they could command. Then, investors erroneously concluded that appreciation in value was intrinsic to real estate in an inflationary economy…regardless of whether rents increased. The image of real estate changed from the income property image which was analogous to **income stocks** like those issued by utilities. The new image was **go go**…like a "growth" stock on Wall Street. "Who needs dividends?" say those who invest in "growth" stocks, "We've got appreciation."

After several years of inflation and rapid property value appreciation, the consensus became, "Real estate will always appreciate."

That's not true. It never was. It only appeared to be so nationally for a relatively brief period in the seventies…and for a longer period in certain markets like California.

But along with inflation came the Nixon wage and price controls of the early seventies. When they were lifted, leftists had tasted rent control "blood" and they liked it. A wave of rent control ordinances passed in the Northeast in the seventies.

When the property-tax-lowering Proposition 13 was being campaigned for in California, someone started saying rents would go down if it passed. A proponent waving a hand-lettered sign to that effect appeared on the cover of *Newsweek* at the time. It **did** pass…and many landlords did indeed lower their rents to try to keep the anonymous promise. But, inevitably, **some** landlords **raised** rents. The media and the politicians went bananas. In the aftermath of Proposition 13, rent control ordinances spread around California.

Apartment owners found some success getting **anti**-rent control laws passed at the state level in the eighties. Such laws now exist in about 20 states.

The eighties added several more extremely powerful forces to the real estate investment equation:

- Tax law changes
- Interest rate fluctuations
- Environmental liability
- Massive overbuilding.

Tax Laws

On August 13, 1981, President Reagan signed the Economic Recovery Tax Act of 1981 into law. That created the 15-year Accelerated Cost Recovery System (ACRS) which was a bonanza for owners of apartments and other rental properties…the **best** tax law for rental property owners in history. I and other experts figured it **raised** the value of apartment buildings about 20%.

But on October 22, 1986, that same President Reagan signed into law the Tax Reform Act of 1986…the **worst** tax law for rental property owners in history. I and other experts figured its elimination of ACRS, institution of the passive loss limits, expansion of the alternative minimum tax, etc., **reduced** the value of apartment buildings and office buildings by 15% to 25%.

Interest rates used to stay the same for years. From 1970 to 1978, conventional mortgage interest rates on existing homes fluctuated between 8.56% and 9.70%. Between 1979 and 1990, they ranged from about 9% to 16.55%. Roughly speaking, a 20% increase in interest rates (say from 10% to 12%) cuts the value of the property by about 20%. That's because when interest rates increase, investors want a higher return from real estate equity and because the amount of the mortgage must be smaller to have the same cash flow with a higher mortgage interest rate.

The eighties also saw **environmental** problems become an extreme threat to all owners of real estate, especially owners of properties other than single-family homes. I used to say the three most important things in real estate were location, location, and location. Now I say they are toxics, toxics, and toxics. Bad location can hurt you badly. But toxics can cost you far more than the purchase price of the building. Ten times the purchase price is fairly common. And you have unlimited personal liability for the cleanup costs regardless of the nonrecourse nature of your financing.

Finally, the eighties saw massive **overbuilding** in many areas, mostly in the oil patch. I personally lost all the money I had made in fifteen years of apartment investing as a result of owning apartments in Texas when the overbuilding occurred in the mid eighties.

The bottom line is that residential properties are no longer the staid, safe appearing investment they once were. Nowadays, you can lose your shirt investing in rental properties...practically overnight. Their image **should** be like the image of such commodity speculations as pork bellies. Unfortunately for most real estate investors, they have not yet figured out how much the investment world has changed. They are still behaving as though it were 1978.

Don't do that. It's the nineties. Stay alert to stay alive financially.

In today's market, you can't buy a residential building on price and terms that give you breakeven or negative cash flow...no matter how grand a "Chamber of Commerce" speech you can make about the economic future of the region in question. If you buy on breakeven or negative cash flow terms, you're a **speculator**, not an investor. You're **hoping** to make a profit, not **arranging** to make one. That's irresponsible behavior. Like putting your life savings on the blackjack tables in Atlantic City.

Calculated risk

Most investors admit to taking risks...but they claim they only take **calculated** risks. I agree that calculated risks are the only kind they **should** be taking. But I **disagree** that the typical real estate investor is limiting his risk to the calculated kind.

Take interest rates. There is no way anyone on earth can predict interest rates. *The Wall Street Journal* asks prominent economists to forecast interest rates for the next six months every six months. The first time they did that, both the actual short- and long-term interest rates were outside the range of **all** the economists. That is, nobody got it right individually. And even the entire group was wrong. And that was only six months!

When a real estate investor buys a rental property using an adjustable rate mortgage (ARM), he's implicitly assuming that he can predict interest rates for the life of the loan. He thinks they'll be low enough that the ARM rate will be cheaper than the alternative fixed rate that was available at the time he got the ARM. That's a pure gamble, not a calculated risk. And if the investor loses the gamble, he's probably finished financially. That's why I call ARMs financial Russian Roulette.

In the nineties, here are some of the risks residential property investors are facing:

- Rent control.
- High interest rates (especially if you have an ARM).
- Liability for property contamination by a currently known toxic.
- Liability for property contamination caused by toxics which will be added to the list in the future.
- Adverse changes in the income tax laws pertinent to apartment buildings.
- Overbuilding.
- Other adverse laws (e.g., requiring employee benefits, giving tenants additional rights).
- Adverse trends in court decisions which expand landlord liability.
- Recession or depression.

A calculated risk taker doesn't mess with risks he can neither control nor forecast.

Can you control or forecast rent-control risk? To a significant degree, yes. I'll tell you how later in the book.

Can you control or forecast interest-rate risk? No way. Get a fixed-rate mortgage only...assumable if you can get it.

Can you control or forecast contamination by currently known toxics? To a significant degree, yes. By an expensive environmental audit. More on that later in the book.

Can you control or forecast contamination for toxics which will be added to the list in the future? Not really. Who would have predicted asbestos, PCBs, radon, chromium, radiation, sick building syndrome, leaking underground storage tanks, etc. as recently as 1983? I bought an apartment building then and financed it with a Federal Home Loan Mortgage Corporation mortgage. Now, they require environmental audits. Then, they did not.

Undoubtedly, the list of toxics will grow longer in the near future. But we can only guess what will be added. Fiberglass? Lead solder on copper pipes? Copper? Electric power lines? Chlordane used to kill termites years ago? Lawn fertilizer used over the years? Landscape pesticides used years ago? Vinyl? Caulk?

Can you control or forecast changes in income tax law? Are you kidding? The Tax Reform Act of 1986 shocked even Congressional leaders when it came out of the Senate Finance Committee in May of that year.

Can you control or forecast overbuilding? You can see what's in the pipeline to come on line in the next 18 months or so if you make the effort. Most investors don't make the effort. And in view of the many other variables that can hurt you even in the absence of too much building, the investors who don't make the effort are probably right albeit for the wrong reason (laziness).

Can you control or forecast the passage of adverse laws other than tax laws? Sometimes you get months' or years' notice as the laws are being debated in Congress. Although by then, the prospective buyers of your building are also aware of the pending law and they accordingly offer less for your building.

Can you control or forecast court trends which expand landlord liability? Well, the trend in the last twenty years is clear. The courts are looking for any excuse to hold the landlord liable for any real or imagined harm suffered by a tenant or visitor to the property or even near the property.

Lawsuits

I recently went to trial in a case in which one of my tenants was raped and blamed me. I lost. Even though the tenant told the court that her pin lock worked and told police she had not used the pin lock on her sliding glass door the night of the rape, the judge said I was 50% at fault for not providing a "workable" pin lock. He also said I was liable for not providing an adequate perimeter security fence (at a garden apartment complex), not providing adequate lights (no one had ever complained about the lights in fifteen years of the building's existence and a lighting expert said we exceeded standards set by the two national standards bureaus).

In my opinion, there is no way I could have avoided liability in that case. The plaintiff cried in the court room. The judge felt sorry for her. The plaintiff's attorneys got into the court the fact that I was insured even though it's not supposed to be allowed. If I had the world's best fence, lighting, sliding glass door locks, the judge would have held me liable for some other reason like not having a full-time security guard.

Can you control or forecast a recession or depression? Nope. I've been expecting a recession for the last seven years. So have a lot of others. The financial graveyards of the world are littered with the bodies of those who thought they could buy at the bottom and sell at the top.

What to do?

If so many crucial factors in residential property success are beyond your ability to control or forecast them, how do you invest in apartments?

In recent years, I've been advocating three investment strategies in my newsletter, *Real Estate Investor's Monthly*:

• Buy for at least 20% less than market value.
• Buy only property that can be upgraded (many ways, not just renovation) profitably.
• Buy only in regions of the country where the normal deal is cheap enough to provide positive cash flow.

It would be inappropriate for me to go into great detail on those strategies here. You can get the bargain purchase strategies by buying back and future issues of my newsletter and by buying my cassette program, "How to Buy Real Estate for at Least 20% Below Market Value." You can get the upgrading strategies from my book, *How to Increase the Value of Real Estate*. And I report on parts of the country where positive cash flow is the norm from time to time in my newsletter.

Anchorage offered positive cash flow during 1989. Reportedly prices have increased there so that's no longer the case. I've also written about Memphis, Oklahoma City, Cleveland, Terre Haute, Johnstown and Lancaster, PA in recent years. Notably absent from my list are such "bargain meccas" as Texas, Colorado, and Arizona. My sources tell me those areas simply never got cheap enough in spite of distressed rental markets of biblical proportions.

At the moment, few markets offer positive cash flow as the norm. And the markets where that's true change. Generally, they are somewhat off-the-beaten path markets that people have given up on. The world never gave up on Texas, Colorado, or Arizona. The market was always sure they'd be back eventually. As long as people have that faith, it's hard to find bargains.

Don't rely on market-wide appreciation

Note that none of my recommended strategies depends on market-wide appreciation for profit. If market-wide appreciation occurs while you own the property, you benefit and I'm happy for you. But if it doesn't, you still make money as a result of your bargain purchase or upgrading or positive cash flow. And if things go badly, either in your market (like a recession) or just in your property (like toxic contamination), you'll lose less than a breakeven or negative cash flow speculator would.

Indeed, one strategy I recommend is deedless investing. That's where you make money in buildings without ever owning one. For example, you might acquire an option to buy a tenant-in-common interest at a big discount (See "Partial Interests" in my February and March 1989 newsletters). Then you ask the other tenants in common if they would rather buy you out at a profit or face a partition lawsuit (in which you have a court force the sale of the property).

In that deal, you'd make a big profit...without ever owning the property. If property values declined because of higher interest rates or recession or whatever, you wouldn't care because you were only exposed to such things very briefly and indirectly through your option. And if some future owner or the government is hit with a huge toxic liability and tries to sue all the former owners, your name will not appear in the chain of title.

By holding the property for only a short period of time...as long as it takes to get the benefit of your bargain...or as long as it takes to complete the upgrading...you minimize your exposure to overbuilding and lawsuits and all that.

And if you insist on investing in the old-fashioned way...that is buying and holding for five or ten years...buying at a bargain price or a property with upgrading potential or a property with positive cash flow will give you a shock-absorbing equity or cash-flow cushion in the event bad things happen in the future.

2

Homeowners Associations

Part of the package

When you buy a condo or a group of condos in the same building as investors sometimes do, you get a homeowners association whether you like it or not. There are homeowners associations and there are homeowners associations. A problem-ridden homeowners association can infect your finances. Avoid them.

Usually a poor investment

Actually, I recommend that you avoid condos altogether unless you can buy them for at least 20% below current market value. Condos are **chronically overbuilt** in virtually all markets.

In an article I wrote for the May 1988 issue of my newsletter, *Real Estate Investor's Monthly* ("Condo investment return well behind houses"), I said that in market after market, you could find houses which had gone up in value across the street from condos which had not or which had gone up much less.

- A 4/25/88 *BusinessWeek* story said western ski-area condo values had fallen 11% to 58%.

- The Arlington, VA tax assessor said houses there went up in value 16% in 1987 but condos only went up 9%.

- The Boston-area average condo price fell from $160,592 in July 1988 to $150,418 in November 1988.

- The DC Board of Realtors® said house prices there went **up** 4% in 1987 but that condo prices went **down** 4% in the same period.

- The San Fernando Board of Realtors® (California) said house prices there went up 18.4% between March 1987 and March 1988; condo prices, only 2.8%.

- The average regional appreciation rates reported by the National Association of Realtors® for condos and co-ops were lower than those for houses every year but 1982…a year in which record high interest rates drove many would-be house buyers to condos in the West.

- Nationally syndicated real estate columnist Robert Bruss asked his 500-newspaper reading audience if any of them knew anyone who systematically (rather than occasionally) made money investing in condos. He got one letter…from a banker who had foreclosed condos to **sell**.

Sue the builder

Homeowners associations are involved in more than their share of litigation. The reason they are often plaintiffs is that small grievances which would normally not be litigated by individuals are big enough to pay attorneys fees when aggregated. So the typical new condo is suing its builder for various construction defects. Unfortunately for the condo owners in that development, the litigation slanders the condos thereby hurting their resale values.

Early in my career, I attended a condo homeowners association meeting because I was selling condos and wanted to know more about them. I took notes on a steno pad. The meeting was amazing with condo owners hurling wild accusations of "malfeasance and misfeasance" at the volunteer board of directors and much wailing and gnashing of teeth about countless construction defects.

A number of condo owners noticed my note taking and assumed I was a news reporter. They then implored me to tell my readers what a rotten guy the builder was and what a rotten job he had done building their condo development. I explained that I was not a reporter and pointed out to them that it was not in their interest to bad mouth the development because they were now its owners and that the negative publicity they were so eager to get would undoubtedly do far more damage to their property values than it could possibly do to the builder.

Unfortunately for would-be condo owners, they would have none of my suggestion that they lighten up. They were so consumed with hatred for the builder that they were totally uninterested in the effect their exaggerated complaints were having on their property value. That sort of self-destructive behavior seems to be the norm in homeowners associations.

Sue the homeowners association

Most people are reluctant to sue their neighbor…even when they have a case they would probably win in court. But homeowners associations…which are typically corporations…now that's another story. Suing impersonal corporations with all their insurance and money, well, that's a popular activity in America today.

Suits may hurt individual condo owners in spite of the association's insurance coverage in two ways:

- A settlement or judgment larger than the policy limit.
- The threat of such an settlement or judgment in a pending suit.

If litigation is already ongoing, and there is a possibility of a greater-than-policy-limit liability, the litigation will depress resale value. Such lawsuits are typically publicized in the local press and are therefore known to local real estate agents who are required to disclose such things.

Homeowners associations can be sued by a visitor whose child drowns or suffers brain damage in the condo pool. Or by condo owners whose unit has some real or imagined problem caused by action or inaction on the part of the association's officers. Or by anyone who is assaulted on or near homeowners association property. Or by property owners who own property adjacent to or near the homeowners association's property. The possibilities are limited only by the imaginations of plaintiffs' attorneys…an extraordinarily imaginative bunch.

Guilt by association

Sometimes, you can't sell your condo because of homeowners association problems which do **not** involve litigation. For example, I know of one condo where the surveyor had made an error. When it was discovered, none of the condos in that development could get title insurance. That, in turn, meant the owners of those condos could neither refinance nor sell them at all.

In another condo I know of, three units slid part way down a hill. The slide would not have affected neighboring units if they had been unrelated houses. But because they were all part of the same homeowners association and the association had to pay to fix the houses (it sued the builder), condos in that development were unsaleable for years.

In yet another condo I'm familiar with, the condo owners decided they did not need to save money for replacement of capital items like the roof and pavement. They figured they'd just ante up the full amount of the money as needed. They were $7,000 per unit below guidelines when I heard about it. Unfortunately, lenders refuse to make mortgages in condos where the homeowners association does not have sufficient funds in its reserve and replacement accounts. The lack of available mortgages caused condos in that development to sell for $20,000 to $25,000 per unit below normal market value.

Of course, lenders don't worry about such things at all in detached single-family house lending unless the need to replace the roof or pavement or whatever is imminent.

Investor-owned units

Investor-owned condos are usually a problem. FHA won't make loans in condo developments where investor- rather than occupant-owned units exceed a certain percentage. An experienced condo manager I interviewed says investor owners always vote against all dues increases thereby causing condo developments with a significant percentage of investor owners to deteriorate.

Tenants also are harder on the common areas than owner occupants.

And investor owners of condos frequently tell their tenants to call the homeowners association if they need any maintenance. In fact, the homeowners association only takes care of **common area** maintenance. Maintenance **inside** an individual unit is the responsibility of the owner of the individual unit. The erroneous instruction to call the association on all maintenance results in delayed maintenance which often results in more extensive damage including damage to common areas caused by water leaking from individual units or some such.

Questions to ask:

The following questions should be asked of a homeowners association board member. The longer the person's tenure on the board, the better.

• Is the association currently involved in any litigation? _____

_____

• Is the association contemplating initiating any litigation? _____

_____

• Has anyone threatened the association with litigation? _____

_____

• Does the association property have any water more than one foot deep like swimming pools, lake, pond, stream, etc.? _____

_____

• Does the association have a playground? _____

_____

• Does the association have any fences? _____

_____

• Does the association employ security guards? _____

_____

Water, playgrounds, fences, and security guards are prime personal-injury lawsuits magnets.

• Does the association have a reserve and replacement fund? _____

_____

• Does the amount in the fund equal or exceed pertinent guidelines given the ages of the property's major capital items? _____

_____

• Have you heard of any title problems involving association property? _____

_____

• Have you heard of any condo owner having trouble selling their unit? _____

_____

• If so, what was the nature of the problem? _____

_____

• Have you ever heard of any condo owner or buyer having trouble getting financing for a condo unit in this development? _____

_____

• What percentage of the units in the development are rented? _____

_____

• May I look at the homeowners association newsletters for the last two years?

_____

• When is the next homeowners association meeting scheduled? _____

_____

• What have the homeowners association dues been each year? _____

_____

• How much are the dues expected to be next year? _____

_____

Additional homeowners association notes:

PART TWO:
<u>LOCATION</u>

3

Neighborhood

The old saying was that the three most important things in real estate were **location, location, and location. Toxics** are more important now. But location is still extremely important. The reason is, you can't fix it.

It's bad enough that you sometimes can't tell when a currently good neighborhood is going to go bad in the future. You sure as heck don't want to make the even worse mistake of **starting out** with a bad neighborhood that you could have avoided if you had paid adequate attention at acquisition.

What's a bad neighborhood?

What's a bad neighborhood? There's no clear-cut definition.

In theory, **no** neighborhood is a bad investment if you get the property cheaply enough. For example, the neighborhood may be so undesirable that a one-bedroom apartment rents for $100 a month. Is that a place to avoid?

Well, if you could buy the building for, say, $3,600 a unit, it'd be a heck of an investment. With a mortgage of $2,400 a unit at 11%, your monthly mortgage payments would be $22.86 per unit. If your operating expenses were, say, 55% of the gross income or $55 a month, you'd have positive cash flow of $100 - $55 - $22.86 = $22.14 per unit per month or $265.68 per year. Not a bad return on your $1,200 investment (22% actually).

Reality

The problem with the theory is reality can change the numbers or make them **unpredictable**. For example, it's hard to get good employees or contractors to work in bad neighborhoods. It's hard to get good tenants to live in bad neighborhoods. So your bad-neighborhood building with the projected 22% cash-on-cash return may perform far worse because you can't find tenants who can be relied upon to pay the $100 rent…or employees or contractors who can be relied upon to collect the rent, fix the broken faucets, etc. necessary to maintain the 55% operating expense ratio.

Outside contractors may refuse to work there. A friend of mine became the supervisor of a slum apartment building in Oakland by taking a new job. His new company had invested its employee pension fund in a second mortgage on a slummy building. The borrower defaulted and the pension fund foreclosed. Their credit bid of the second mortgage amount was the high bid so they became the owners of the building. They immediately tried to hire a property manager. No property manager would accept the property. Furthermore, no plumber would work there. And so forth. They were completely unable to manage the property at all.

They ended up selling the property so cheap that they lost the **entire** $100,000 they had invested in the mortgage.

Here's an item from Donald Trump's book, *The Art of the Deal*, on the subject of collecting rents from apartments his father owned in bad neighborhoods.

> *One of the first tricks I learned was that you never stand in front of someone's door when you knock. Instead you stand by the wall and reach over to knock. The first time a rent collector explained that to me, I couldn't imagine what he was talking about. "What's the point?" I said. He looked at me like I was crazy. "The point," he said, "is that if you stand to the side, the only thing exposed to danger is your hand." I still wasn't sure what he meant. "In this business," he said, "if you knock on the wrong apartment at the wrong time, you're liable to get shot."*

Donald decided, "…my father's scene was a little rough for my tastes." And for mine…and I hope, yours.

Flying blind

What's the operating expense ratio on a building no employee or outside contractor will set foot into? You're in a whole different world, aren't you?

Later in the book, I'll tell you to use regional or national income/expense studies to estimate the unverifiable portion of your operating statement. But those figures are generally based on surveys of buildings in **good** neighborhoods. So those figures are only valid in **similar** neighborhoods. In **slum** neighborhoods you are going in somewhat blind because of the lack of reliable operating data on slum properties.

So the more accurate financial picture of such a property may be:

• The rents are $100 a month…**if** you can get anyone to A, move in, and B, pay it.

• The operating expense ratio is **unknown** because normal people won't work there. The few who will, will charge amounts which are high and unpredictable.

- This building will require enormous amounts of the owner's **time** because he'll have to do so much himself and the tenants will generally either be childlike or criminals...both of whom require extraordinary amounts of supervision.

It's all relative

In New York City, people pay high rents to live in crime-infested, run-down neighborhoods. Or at least what **non**-New Yorkers would call crime-infested, run-down neighborhoods. New Yorkers and other city dwellers often put up with levels of crime and disrepair which cause suburbanites to push their car's lock buttons down and head for the hills.

The key is **predictability**. If you can get reliable operating data and reliable tenants, employees, and outside contractors for the building in question, you ought to be able to analyze it by investment criteria and make your decision whether to buy or not based on the price, terms, and likely profit performance of the property. In New York, you probably can get reliable data and people to work on such buildings.

Drug forfeiture

Another risk which has arisen in recent years for residential landlords is the risk that the police will seize your property on the grounds that illegal activities like drug dealing are occurring there. Under the Comprehensive Crime Control Act of 1984, forfeiture is automatic if the property owner knew of or consented to the illegal use. Some municipalities like Portland, Oregon, have even stricter laws.

If you buy in high-crime neighborhoods, police seizure risk is increased.

Crime

How can you tell if a neighborhood has a high crime rate? Ask the **police**.

I used to think I could tell by driving around the neighborhood. That was before I bought in what I thought was a nice neighborhood. Before two of my tenants were raped and one sued me. At the trial, the police testified that my building's neighborhood had the second highest crime rate in Fort Worth!

Essentially, if your tenants or visitors to your building become crime victims, you will likely be sued. Not every time. But too often.

And you will **lose** the lawsuit. Taking precautions and more-than-reasonable care won't help. Once the crime occurs, you're liable regardless of your carefulness. That's not what the law says. But it is the *de facto* way the law is interpreted today. So the main way to avoid liability is to avoid buying in neighborhoods where crime is a problem.

Drive around

In addition to checking with the police, you should do your own drive around. Reject the neighborhood if it looks bad in **either** the police figures or the drive around. Here are some things to look for in a drive around:

- What percentage of walls have graffiti? _____

- What percentage of properties have bars on windows? _____

• What percentage of stores have steel grates across display windows when closed?

_____

• What percentage of stores have signs with messages for criminals like, "Manager cannot open safe"? _____

• Is there a municipal curfew law (often posted on signs)?_____

In the area where I live, the San Ramon Valley in California, virtually none of the properties have bars, grates, graffiti, or signs for criminals. The San Ramon Valley, as far as I know, is a low-crime area. In the Fort Worth area where I bought the property that later became a rape scene, I was satisfied to see that "only" about 5% of the homes had bars on the windows during my pre-purchase drive around. I now know that even 5% is too many.

Lack of interest by property insurers

During the nationwide insurance crisis of the mid eighties, my insurance on the Fort Worth building was cancelled. A nationally known insurance company with offices right down the street refused to quote a premium on the property. Through a consultant who worked with an agent in another city, I ended up getting insurance with that same company after all. But I suspect that the local office refused because of the crime rate. If, in the process of investigating a prospective acquisition, you have any trouble getting insurance agents to bid on the property, look out. Check the crime rate and other possible factors closely before you proceed.

Signs of economically weak neighborhood

The main economic thing you want to know when checking a neighborhood in connection with a prospective rental acquisition is the fair-market-rental value of the units. And you do that by checking comparable units and talking to rental agents. But you can also get clues as to the economic health of the neighborhood from the following:

• Percentage of vacant stores? _____

• Percentage of stores rented to charitable organizations? _____

> **Charities pay little or no rent. They are not much better than vacancies.**

• Number of "adult" sex-oriented stores? _____

• Names of national chains or franchises represented (like McDonalds, 7-11, etc.)

National chains and franchises have sophisticated analysts to determine where to put their outlets. The more there are in the neighborhood you're interested in, the better.

"Prime" neighborhoods

Many real estate investors believe that so-called "prime" neighborhoods are the best place to invest. Not really. In fact, they may be one of the **worst**.

An investor seeks a return on his investment. The highest return he can get consistent with the risk he is willing to take. The best investment, therefore, is the one with the highest return and an acceptable risk.

In recent history, return on real estate has come from:

• Cash flow
• Appreciation
• Tax savings
• Amortization.

The best cash-flow return comes from the highest capitalization rate combined with the lowest loan constant. The capitalization rate is the net operating income divided by property price. Net operating income is rent minus all expenses except mortgage payments. For a homeowner, it would be take-home pay. The loan constant is the annual mortgage payments divided by the loan balance. The problem with buildings in prime locations is that they typically have **low** cap rates, not high ones. The reason is, simply, that the **buyers** of such buildings are more impressed with them than the **tenants** are.

For example, Snob Hill Estates may rent for $800 a month because it's in a "prime" neighborhood. While Average Apartments, which is in an average neighborhood, rents for just $400 a month. Which is the better investment?

We can't tell until we hear the price. Typically, Snob Hill would sell for something like **two and a half times** what Average Apartments would sell for. But wait a minute. Snob Hill is obviously more desirable for tenants. It rents for **twice** as much as Average Apartments. But **only** twice as much. **Not** two and a half times as much.

Let's say Average Apartments would sell for $36,000 a unit and Snob Hill for $90,000 a unit. Based strictly on income, the **price** differential ought to match the **rent** differential. That is, if Average Apartments rent for $400 a month and sell for $36,000 a unit, Snob Hill ought to sell for $72,000 a unit (double the price of Average Apartments) because its rents are double those of Average Apartments. So what does the buyer of Snob Hill who pays a premium of $90,000 - $72,000 = $18,000 get for his $18,000? Bragging rights.

Investors who buy properties in "prime" locations are called "pride-of-ownership" investors by real estate agents. Put more bluntly, they are show offs. They want to own the "prime" property so they can mention it in conversations, find excuses to stop there when they have friends or relatives in the car, etc.

I find that a waste of money. But it is quite common.

Less risk, more appreciation?

Pride of ownership investors protest that "prime" locations are **worth** the premium because they are less risky and they appreciate more.

Not true.

For example, in 1982, the highest priced homes in America were in Anaheim, CA ($133,000). Louisville, KY homes were lowest priced at $46,000. Anaheim was the more "prime" location and therefore the best investment, right?

Wrong.

In 1985, Anaheim homes sold for $136,200; Louisville, for $50,600. The annual appreciation rate in Anaheim was 0.8%. In Louisville, it was 3.0%. If you had bought a million dollars worth of homes in Anaheim instead of Louisville you'd have missed out on a lot of profit. In Louisville, your $1,000,000 would have bought 21.74 houses each of which went up $50,600 - $46,000 = $4,600 for a profit of 21.74 x $4,600 = $100,004. But in "prime" Anaheim, you'd have bought only 7.52 homes and made only $3,200 per home for a total of $24,060. That's $100,004 - $24,060 = $75,944 in profit lost because you insisted on buying "prime" property.

The Anaheim/Louisville comparison is a **national** one. But you can get similar results looking at **local** numbers. For example, the *San Francisco Chronicle* occasionally runs an article on median home prices in the San Francisco Bay Area. The March 28, 1988 edition listed the percentage price increase for most Bay Area suburbs. The six **highest**-priced neighborhoods were priced from $289,000 to $425,000 in 1986 and appreciated from 11.76% to 29.41% between 1986 and 1987. But the six **lowest**-priced neighborhoods were priced at $79,000 to $90,000 and appreciated from 13.33% to 56.25%.

High **prices** don't make you any money. High **appreciation rates** do. And high-priced neighborhoods have no monopoly on high appreciation rates.

Buying a "**prime**" apartment building with a $100,000 net operating income for more than you'd pay for an **average** apartment building with the same NOI is like paying extra for a bond with more attractive engraving than another bond with the same coupon interest rate. Or like instructing your bond broker to buy bonds issued in higher **face** amounts...regardless of coupon interest rate...on the theory that they appreciate more. A bond broker you told that to would decline your business on the grounds that you are obviously some kind of nut and need a guardian appointed to take care of your finances.

Cain & Scott income property brokers in Seattle issue an annual *Apartment Market Study*. Their 1988 edition clearly showed that the **higher** the **rents** were in a complex, the **lower** the **cap rates** were. That means the buyers of the nicer buildings were paying extra for the prestige of owning those buildings. That is extremely dumb.

Liquidity

I will grant that "prime" properties are **more liquid** than less desirable properties. That's because the myth of investment superiority distorts the behavior of the marketplace at times. Lenders often cut back by **redlining**. "Prime" neighborhoods are the **last** to get redlined.

Buyers who are **in love** with "prime" neighborhoods pine for them for years and some are always able and willing to buy the targets of their affection even when buyers in general are cutting back.

But liquidity is not yield. Rather it is a temporary advantage which you may or may not ever need. Indeed, it is generally impossible to know in advance that you are going to need liquidity in the future.

And liquidity is not free. If it were, you'd always prefer investments that offered superior liquidity…like Treasury Bills. The price you pay for the liquidity advantage of "prime" properties is the lost cash flow and possibly appreciation those buildings represent compared to less sought-after buildings. A better way to meet reasonable liquidity goals is to arrange lines of credit and/or to have a small part of your net worth in such liquid form as CDs or investment grade securities.

Neighborhood toxics

Toxics on your property are not the only ones you have to worry about. In many cases, property values have been devastated in a wide area because of contamination on a nearby property. Love Canal in New York and Times Beach, Missouri are two of the most notorious examples of neighborhood contamination. There are many more which didn't make the national news but which **did** do severe damage to the affected property owners. For example, twenty-four thousand residents of Fenald, OH received $73 million for property damage that was caused by a nearby uranium processing plant.

The federal Comprehensive Environmental Response, Compensation, and Liability Act makes you liable for contamination on your property even if it emanated from another property. (You may have a law suit against the polluter but good luck turning that into enough money to cover the damage.)

The Federal National Mortgage Association now requires that all properties within a **one-mile radius** be "analyzed" for possible sources of contamination. Obviously, it would be impossible to get the permission of all the property owners within an appropriate radius to inspect their properties. Just as obviously, the cost would be prohibitive even if you **could** get permission. But you or your environmental auditor ought to drive around the neighborhood to note the **current** uses. And you should inquire into **past** uses.

Contaminated businesses

Here's a list of some of the businesses which may have contaminated property:

- auto repair
- building materials companies
- chemical companies
- commercial cleaners
- companies which have a fleet of vehicles
- companies which have underground storage tanks
- companies which use radioactive material
- companies which sell salt
- construction companies
- cosmetic manufacturers
- dry cleaners
- dumps
- farms
- fertilizer sellers or manufacturers
- furniture manufacturers/refinishers
- gas stations
- hospitals
- ink manufacturers
- laboratories of all sorts
- lawn and garden maintenance
- metalworking shops
- mines
- paint stores
- pesticide sellers or manufacturers
- photographic film processors
- plastic manufacturers
- printers
- ranches
- refineries
- upholsterers
- wood preservers

You may say, "Hey, wait a minute. Every neighborhood in America has those businesses!"

True. Welcome to the new age of environmentalism where **all** people rich enough to own investment or business property are guilty of a crime (owning contaminated property)…a crime which entitles the government to confiscate their life savings. Actually, that's overstating it a bit. But it seems to be the direction in which we are moving.

Remember, it's not just present businesses that matter. If any of these businesses were **ever** in the neighborhood, contamination from them may adversely affect your property.

Flood hazard

Low-lying sites are often in flood plains. As part of the National Flood Insurance Program, flood-plain **maps** have been drawn up showing the areas likely to be flooded as a result of extraordinary precipitation. They are rated A (worst) to C (best) or V (coastal). The entire country is in one zone or the other so you probably don't need to worry if the property in question is in a B or C zone. Federally-related lenders don't. They only require flood insurance on loans on properties in A or V zones.

Call the city or county engineer's office to get a copy of the pertinent flood map. Lenders also know how to get flood maps and may have one they can show you. And you can get the maps from the Federal Emergency Management Agency at the Flood Map Distribution Center, 6930 (A-F) San Tomas Road, Baltimore, MD 21227-6227, 800-333-1363.

If the building you are considering is in an A or V flood plain, be careful unless you can get a good deal **and** cover the flood risk with federal flood insurance. There is a top limit on how much flood insurance you can get. For commercial buildings like apartment buildings, the per-building (a building is defined as being separated by "clear intervening space" or a floor-to-roof firewall from other buildings) limit as I write this is $100,000 for areas using the "Emergency" flood program and $250,000 for areas eligible for the "regular" program. Some communities have not met the minimum requirements to be in **either** program so federal flood insurance is not available in those areas at all.

In view of the limit, you need to be careful of buying buildings which have replacement costs **above** $250,000. If the flood risk in question is likely to consist solely of **rising water**, the damage to the building would probably be far less than a total loss. So $250,000 of flood insurance on a $1,000,000 building, for example, may be enough to fully cover the likely loss.

But **raging** water or **ocean waves** can and often do wipe the building and even a lot off the face of the earth. In that case, you are exposing yourself to significant flood risk when you buy a building with a replacement cost above the $250,000 limit.

The normal deductible is $500. There are premium discounts of up to 35% for deductibles up to $5,000. The insurance premiums are higher for the more dangerous A, B, and V areas. Flood insurance is **bare bones coverage** for replacing the building only. You cannot get flood insurance for such other related risks as loss of rents during reconstruction or increased building costs because of stricter building codes passed since the original building was built. So in view of the deductibles and lack of business interruption and other related risk coverage, you are always forced to **self-insure** to an extent when you buy a building in a high-risk flood plain.

• Flood-zone rating of this property: _____

Slide hazard

Federal flood insurance covers slide risk. **Wet** slides, that is. Dry slides are uninsurable as far as I know. Federal flood maps do not indicate slide hazard. If the property in question is neither at the top or bottom of a slope and is level, there probably is **no** slide hazard. When there **is** a slope, you should make appropriate inquiries as to the slide history of the area. Here are some sources:

- Look up slide stories in back indexes of local newspapers.
- Ask long-time merchants or residents in the area.
- Hire soils engineer.

- Slide risk at this property _____

> With slides, total loss is common so make sure the building's replacement cost is within the federal flood insurance policy limit.

Earthquake risk

Earthquake risk varies by neighborhood. Witness the devastation in some blocks of the Marina District of San Francisco in the World Series 1989 earthquake.

Earthquake risk is much like flood risk in that maps and insurance are available. As with floods, it's relatively easy to forecast which buildings will be damaged and in what way. The main unknown is **when** the damage will occur.

Contrary to popular belief, most parts of the United States are earthquake country. The **worst** quake in U.S. history hit **New Madrid, Missouri** on December 16, 1811. **Charleston, South Carolina** had a big quake in 1886 and **Boston**, in the 1700s. Quakes in the middle and eastern parts of the U.S. do damage over a far wider area than the same quake would do in the West because of the underlying geology. Furthermore, because quakes are very infrequent in the middle and eastern parts of the U.S., those areas lack quake-resistant building codes and as a result, quake-resistant buildings.

Before you buy a building in any part of the U.S., you should ascertain the earthquake rating of the underlying land. The U.S. Geological Survey, which has offices in major cities, publishes maps of earthquake risk.

- Earthquake rating of this location _____

Roughly speaking, the same areas with bad flood ratings have bad earthquake ratings. That is, **low ground** is a bad place to be in an earthquake; high ground is much better. That's because fill and silt deposits shake like jello in an earthquake (called liquefaction) and rock (which causes high ground) does not.

The earthquake risk of a particular lot is determined by:

- The nature of the underlying **soil.**
- The distance to the nearest earthquake **fault.**
- The geology and structures **uphill** from your location.

- The distance to and relative elevation of **dams** upstream from your property.
- The architecture of **adjacent** buildings.

If the location in question is subject to significant earthquake risk, you should be careful to ascertain the extent to which you can obtain **earthquake insurance** from a sound, reputable insurance company. You should also take extra precautions to analyze the earthquake resistance of the **structure** and the cost of any modifications that are necessary to bring the building up to reasonable safety standards.

School districts

School districts can have a tremendous effect on the value of residential properties with two or more bedrooms per unit. In his book, *The Builders*, Martin Mayer tells this story.

A builder named Miller Nichols built a housing development in the Kansas City area called the Country Club District. It straddled State Line Road which was, in fact, the border between Kansas and Missouri.

The houses on the two sides of State Line Road still look alike...But in fact you can pick up homes on the Missouri side for ten and twenty percent less than the homes on the Kansas side...If you bring up your children on the Missouri side, you live with the prospect that one of these days the federal court will order your children bused to the unhappy slums of downtown Kansas City for their schooling; but if you live on the Kansas side you're safely in the Shawnee Mission School District, with a high school now rated better than Southwest [High School in Missouri] and with absolute safety because there is no judge with a jurisdiction that extends to both sides of the line.

University Park and Highland Park are prestige communities surrounded by Dallas. In recent years, one of the two was ordered to have its children bused to Dallas schools. A study by appraisers showed that the values of homes in the affected area dropped significantly.

Additional neighborhood notes:

4

How to Avoid Rent Control

Some owners of rent-controlled properties make a profit and are relatively content. In many others, the owners rue the day they bought the building. They and their capital are essentially prisoners of the tenants.

Worst of both worlds

The worst case is when you buy a building at normal prices, then it becomes rent controlled **after** you buy it. In the typical case, the value of the building drops sharply when rent control is imposed. 20% is the figure I've heard most. And then, if the rent control is stringent, i.e., less than cost of living increases and no interim or vacancy decontrol, the building declines further at a gradual rate each year as the net operating income gets smaller and smaller.

Within a couple of years of instituting rent control, most communities find themselves fighting a losing battle to keep owners from getting their property tax assessments reduced because of the falling values of their buildings.

Once rent control is passed, there typically follows a steady stream of related anti-landlord laws. Only a handful of communities which passed rent control have later gotten rid of it…Lynn and Somerville in Massachusetts and Miami Beach (by state law). Someone said of rent control, "It's like heroin: starting is euphoric, quitting is impossible, and continuing is disastrous."

In short, a rent-controlled community is a landlord hell. Buying a building which is already rent controlled is like getting a lung transplant from a lung cancer victim. Buying a building which is likely to become rent controlled is like getting a lung transplant from a heavy smoker. You shouldn't do either.

It's easy to find out if a municipality has rent control. Just ask the city government or the local apartment association.

Identifying municipalities which are **likely** to become rent controlled in the future is harder. But it can be done.

State laws

A number of states have passed laws which forbid rent control or make it a matter which can only be instituted at the state level. That, more or less forbids rent control because no state has ever controlled rents statewide. (Some have passed enabling legislation which permitted municipalities to pass rent control.)

As of this writing, here are the states which have state laws which prohibit or discourage municipal rent control:

Where rent control is prohibited or discouraged by law	
State	Authority
AZ	Title 33, Chapter 3 Article 1 AZ Revised Statutes §33-132-1329, Title 43, Chapter 10, Article 4 ARS §43-1060
CA	(**non**-residential) Title 5, Prt.4, Div.3, CCC Ch.2.6, §1954.25
CO	§1, Article 12, Title 38 CO Revised Statutes 1973, part 3
FL	Chapter 77-50 FS 1985 166.043
GA	Article 1, Chapter 7, Title 44, Code Of GA, § 44-7-19
ID	H.B. 555 (3-28-90)
LA	Chapter 1, Code Title IX, Title 9 LA Revised Statutes 1950 part V RS9:3258
MI	pending Senate Bill 583
MN	Laws of MN Chapter 551 S.F. No. 1683 471.995-6
MO	H.B. 602 (5-18-89)
MS	Senate Bill 2006 (3-16-90)
NC	§1, Chapter 42, General Statutes of NC §42-14.1 (1987)
NH	Girard v. Town of Allenstown, 428 Atlantic Reporter, 2d Series 488 (Supreme Court of NH, 1981)
OK	OK Statutes §14-101.1 of Title 11 (3/21/88)
OR	OR Legislative Assembly House Bill 2505 (1985)
SC	Code Of Laws of SC §27-39-60 (1976)
SD	Senate Bill 260 (2-23-90)
TX	Chapter 472, Act of the 51st Legislature 1949 (Article 12691-1, Vernon Texas Civil Statutes) §1b
UT	§1, Utah Code of 1953, §57-19-1 (1987)
VA	Codes of VA Chapter 13-2 §55-248.3 with §15.1 - 839, 491.8
WA	Chapters 35.21, 36.01 RCW

Sources: National Apartment Association, National Multi Housing Council

Municipal politics

Liberals and **affluent tenants** are the ones who get rent control laws passed. Avoid municipalities which have lots of liberals or affluent tenants and you will avoid municipal rent control.

Does that sound too simplistic? Consider which cities have rent control.

New York City has had it since World War II. Do they have liberals in New York? Is the Pope Catholic?

Berkeley, California has rent control. They have liberals there, too. Only in Berkeley a liberal is considered right wing. I suspect Berkeley is secretly a member of the Warsaw Pact.

Santa Monica has rent control. They did a story about it on *60 Minutes*. The name of the story was "The People's Republic of Santa Monica."

Here are the names of some other cities which have rent control along with the Americans for Democratic Action (ADA) ratings of their congresspersons and the percentage which voted for the Democratic presidential candidate in the '84 election. (ADA is the quintessential liberal organization. The more ADA likes a Congressperson's votes, the closer his or her rating is to 100%.)

City	Congressman	ADA Rating	'84 %Demo
DC	Fauntroy	non-voting	85%
Boston	Markey	95%	49%
	Kennedy	new	64%
	Moakley	95%	51%
Brookline, MA	Frank	100%	51%
San Francisco	Pelosi	new	65%

Other liberal indicators

Election results are the best indicators. Just look for elections where liberals tended to favor one side. Here are some elections where liberals voted overwhelmingly for one side:

1972 Presidential election   (Nixon vs. McGovern)
1978 Proposition 13 in California   (tax revolt)
1980 Presidential election   (Reagan vs. Carter)
1984 Presidential election   (Reagan vs. Mondale)
1988 Presidential election   (Bush vs. Dukakis)

Tax revolts in other states would be good indicators like California's Proposition 13.

To get the election results, go to a library and look up the local newspaper for the day after the election or the day after that. They typically break the results down by municipality. Municipalities which give extraordinary numbers of votes to liberal causes or candidates...even if less than a majority...are municipalities which are likely to pass rent control ordinances in the future.

Recent elections are best but it probably does not matter. The areas which voted for McGovern in '72 (DC and Boston) are still liberal. The political nature of an area changes glacially over centuries. (The vote of the Massachusetts legislature to symbolically exempt Massachusetts citizens from serving in the Vietnam war was not the first time for such a declaration. It had been done in one of America's wars over a hundred years before. By which state? Massachusetts.)

Colleges are also liberal bastions. There are some rural areas in California which are ostensibly populated by nothing but redwoods and rednecked lumberjacks. Yet they have had rent control battles. Upon further examination, one finds that the community in question is home to a state college.

Winston Churchill once observed that,

If a man is not a liberal when he is twenty, he has no heart. If he is not a conservative when he is forty, he has no brain.

College students tend to be about twenty and, therefore, can be forgiven for the fact that they are also generally liberal politically. College professors are not twenty but they are darned sure liberal. Both the students and their professors have excess time on their hands so they can and often do devote the time needed to get rent control passed.

Senior citizens are not liberal as a group. But they have developed a the-world-owes-me-a-discount mentality in recent years. They also have lots of time on their hands for campaigning. So you often find rent control ordinances which apply to mobilehome parks...a predominantly senior-occupied housing type.

Affluent tenants

Rent control proponents claim they want to help the poor. In fact, tenants of **all** income levels want rent control.

Affluent tenants are more dangerous to landlords because they know how to get what they want.

I discovered the affluent tenants danger signal when I was listing all the rent-controlled communities I could think of to see if they were, indeed, liberal politically. One was not: Cherry Hill, New Jersey.

Cherry Hill voted for Nixon in '72. It had no college. No mobilehome park concentration. So who got rent control passed?

Cherry Hill has lots of high-rise apartment buildings. High-rise apartment buildings which are not government-owned are invariably occupied by affluent tenants. High-rise apartment buildings are a political organizers' dream. You can leaflet the entire building in a matter of minutes without going outside. You can communicate almost effortlessly to virtually every tenant by simply putting a notice up in the elevators. And, in Cherry Hill at least, the politicians actually put voting booths in the lobbies of the high-rises on voting day.

When I was a tenant in a high-rise in San Francisco, the usual activists tried for years to get rent control passed. It lost every time. Then my landlord, who had a total of 1,500 high-rise units around the city, raised all the rents by about 55%. San Francisco had rent control in three weeks.

Dick Van Dyke lived in that building when I moved out. I ran into actor David Jansen in the lobby once. Liberace stayed down the hall one night. I also used to see San Francisco Mayor George Moscone going to parties in the building at times. Many of these tenants had the **private numbers** of the mayor and city supervisors in their Rolodexes. Armies of poor and middle class tenants clamored for rent control in San Francisco for years to no avail. But the affluent got it almost overnight.

Want more evidence of the ability and inclination of affluent tenants to get rent control? Look at some of the towns that **have** rent control. Would you believe Beverly Hills and Palm Springs? And look at the towns that do **not** have rent control...like Philadelphia and Detroit.

Tenant majorities

If you want to avoid future rent control, do not invest in towns with tenant majorities. Here are some rent-controlled communities and their percentage of tenants as of the 1970 census:

New York City	77.0%
Boston	74.5%
DC	73.4%
Cambridge, MA	81.3%
Newark, NJ	80.5%

Summary

To avoid having your apartment acquisition become rent controlled:

- Buy in states with state anti-rent-control laws.
- Do **not** buy in communities which have:
  - Tenant majorities.
  - Liberal majorities.
  - Concentration of senior citizens.
  - Privately-owned, high-rise, apartment buildings.
  - More than 100 tenants with incomes above the national median.

You can find out all of these things in the library of the community in question. Check the Census and other similar books for percentage of home owners and tenants, ages, and incomes. Check old newspapers for voting patterns. And look out the window for high-rises. Or in the "apartments for rent" part of the classified section of the local newspaper.

PART THREE:
FINDING BUILDINGS

5

How to Find Buildings to Buy

Most people's first experience with buying real estate is buying a single-family home. When they decide to buy a rental property, they assume the process is essentially the same, except you look in a different part of the newspaper and go to a different real estate broker.

Not true. Buying rental property is radically different from buying a home. And much more difficult. For starters, you will probably have to approach owners directly...owners who have not said they want to sell...to see enough property. Just responding to ads and going to brokers is almost never enough.

Direct mail

Last time I bought apartments, I sent a letter to all the apartment brokers and all the apartment association members who owned buildings of the size I could afford. Here's what the letter to **brokers** said:

```
Dear Investment Sales Manager:

On September 19, 19xx, I will fly to Dallas to find an
apartment building to buy. For tax reasons, I must close the
purchase on November 1, 1983. I have $160,000 in cash
```

to be used as a 25% down payment. So I want a building in the $600,000 to $650,000 price range.
I ll be staying at the Marriott Quorum, 14901 Dallas Parkway from September 18th until September 25th. The phone number there is 214-661-2800. I am determined to buy a property during that week.

This will be my third one-week acquisition trip to Dallas. On both previous trips, I bought buildings: one for $400,000 in 1978 and one for $600,000 this year. In both cases, the sellers paid real estate commissions.

If you have any apartment buildings in the $600,000 to $650,000 price range, please contact me. My California phone number is 415-555-1362. I will be doing nothing but looking for property during my stay in Dallas. And I will make a signed offer with deposit check on the first acceptable building I see.

Thank you,

John T. Reed

The letter to owners was the same except that the last sentence in the third paragraph was changed to:

I am not a real estate agent so you will save the commission if you sell direct to me.

Please note the following in the letter:

• It's mailed eleven days before my trip.

• The first paragraph states that I am in a hurry and gives the reason I'm in a hurry. That's important because the real estate world is full of tire-kickers and lookers who are not really in a buying mode. Agents are constantly identifying and ignoring such people. Owners often do.

• I state my cash available and percentage down payment up front. A lot of buyers try to pretend they're bigger than they are...probably for ego reasons. That's dumb. The other side will inevitably find out how much cash you have if you buy so why waste time...or more importantly...why risk the seller or agent's thinking maybe you aren't qualified?

• It tells exactly where I'm staying, when, and the phone number so owners and agents can take action if they have a property.

• The third paragraph tries to prove I'm for real. And it deals with the issue of real estate commission which is *sine qua non* to agents and extremely important to owners.

- It encourages the recipient to contact me **before** my departure if they wish.

- It emphasizes several times that I am a serious buyer with the cash, experience, and motivation to do a deal **now**.

- Note the vow to buy the "first acceptable building" in the last paragraph. That's a crucial concept. Most inexperienced or occasional investors think you acquire by looking at several properties and buying the **best** deal. Wrong. You look at properties until you find an **acceptable** deal. Then you buy that one. If you try to accumulate several acceptable deals then pick the best, you'll find faster buyers are beating you out every time. Good deals won't sit still while you try to find two more good deals. Buy the **first** acceptable deal. **Not** the **best** deal. What's an acceptable deal? You should have a written page of criteria before you start to look. When the property in question comes up yes on each criterion, make an offer on it.

All of those things are extremely important when it comes to getting agents to expend any effort on you. They are also helpful to get sellers to take action. That is, they present the owner...who may not have been in a selling mode...with an opportunity which will be gone in a few weeks.

Mailing list

To whom do you mail your letters?

I sent my broker letters to companies whose *Yellow Pages* ad in the Dallas and Fort Worth phone books indicated they sold apartment buildings. And I sent the owner letter to persons or companies listed in the Dallas/Tarrant County Apartment Association Membership Directory. That directory lists all the apartment buildings owned by members and the number of units in each. I mailed to owners whose number of units in the building looked like it would be in my price range.

I did not use, but could have, the more comprehensive *Roddy Apartment Ownership Guide* (214-248-9186). It gives property characteristics and has the name and address of the owners of **all** apartment buildings whether or not they are members of the apartment association. (In the Dallas/Fort Worth area in 1985, about a third of all apartment owners were members of the apartment association.)

Other sources you could use include:

- Local Board of Realtors® directories (for names of agents).
- Certified Commercial-Investment Member (CCIM) of the Realtors® National Marketing Institute directories.
- Membership lists of local real estate investors associations.
- Mailing list brokers (listed under "mailing lists" in the *Yellow Pages*).

If the local real estate investors association has meetings or a newsletter (most have both), ask if they will announce your interest in buying a building at the next meeting and/or in the next newsletter.

It's cheap

The main point is that you have to contact **every single owner** (in your price range) and **every single apartment broker**. That's not as hard as it sounds. The number of apartment owners in a metropolitan area is typically only in the hundreds. And the number who own buildings of the size you want to buy is probably in the dozens. As is the number of apartment building brokers. So you're only talking about sending out about 100 letters. At 25¢ postage each, that's just $25. With secretarial and stationery costs added, the total cost would be less than $200.

Real estate buyers...especially those who have only bought houses...aren't used to putting out money up front to **find** property. Rather they expect to be picked up at the airport and chauffeured around for free by real estate agents who hope to get a commission from the seller. I have been picked up at the airport and chauffeured around by an apartment broker. In fact, that's how I bought the $600,000 apartment building mentioned above.

But today's market is highly competitive in terms of investors fighting each other for good deals. So you can't rely totally on agents.

Rather than look at the $200 expense of the direct mail campaign in contrast to the seller-pays-all house market, compare the $200 to the amount you're planning to spend on the apartment building. Would you spend $200 to improve your chances of getting a better deal on a $600,000 apartment building? I certainly hope so.

Newspapers

You may be able to use newspapers and other periodicals in two ways:

• Monitor the newspaper **classified for sale ads**, e.g., the Friday *Wall Street Journal*, local newspapers, and some trade journals. You're looking for two things: properties and real estate firms which sell apartment buildings. This may seem redundant after you've contacted every owner by direct mail. It's still necessary because the addresses on your mailing lists will be inaccurate or out-of-date. Also, redundancy can be another word for persistence which often makes a deal

• **Property-wanted ads**. They run in the paper continuously. So they must be working for someone. Virtually all property wanted ads say the same things:

  • Quick action
  • No commission
  • All cash
  • Will buy anything
  • No inspections.

That last item: no inspections, is unacceptably accommodating. The people who run the ads say that to get as many sellers as possible to call. But anyone smart enough to buy and use this book is committing fraud if he advertises "no inspections" or colossal stupidity if he actually buys real estate without inspecting it.

Two other recent buzz words have been effective in property-wanted ads:

  • Foreign buyers, and
  • Starker buyer.

"Starker buyer" means the guy running the ad is trying to do a delayed, tax-free exchange and is therefore in a hurry to meet the 45-day deadline for identifying the property to be acquired. Starker was the name of the man whose court case established the right of taxpayers to do delayed exchanges (602 F 2d 1341). The 45-day deadline is in section 1031(a)(3)(A) of the Internal Revenue Code. If you are foreign or in a Starker exchange, by all means use those phrases in your property-wanted ad. (For more information on Starker exchanges, read my book called *Aggressive Tax Avoidance for Real Estate Investors*.)

Classified ads are relatively cheap. About ten bucks a day in the *San Francisco Chronicle* if you run it for twelve days. Or you could only run it once a week in the main real estate section. If it got you one good deal, the expense would easily be worth it.

Jay Kaplan says his former company, Consolidated Capital, used property-wanted ads extensively. He said they only did one deal out of 400 as a direct result of the ads. But another 200 deals resulted from relationships which began with a response to their property-wanted ad. The only paper they found worthwhile was the Friday *Wall Street Journal*.

No secrets

It's hard to find good buildings. People sometimes ask me what the secret is. No secret. Shoe leather mostly. And an altered state of mind.

Altered state of mind

Many activities require an altered state of mind for success. For example, when I was a radio disk jockey in college I discovered that you had to adopt a cheerful demeanor when you went on the air...regardless of how rotten your day had been...or your show would sound terrible.

Athletic activities also require an altered state of mind. To hit a target...as in golf or archery or tennis or baseball batting...turning over the control of your body to your **subconscious** mind works best. Catching a ball...as in baseball fielding or football pass receiving...requires intense **concentration** and awareness. And contact sports like football or hockey or boxing require an artificial **rage**. In contact sports, you either turn yourself into a raving maniac...or you get run over by someone who did.

Real estate acquisition is a "contact sport"

The normal state of mind that gets you through your day-to-day activities will **not** work in real estate acquisitions. Unless you're in another line of work which requires the contact-sport mentality...like real estate sales or labor negotiations.

Doing real estate deals requires a state of mind like the one summed up in this Buxton quote.

...invincible determination of purpose once fixed and then death or victory.
Sir Thomas Buxton

If you try to buy a building through a casual, deliberate process, you won't succeed. You must almost get angry...at the sellers who want too much, the real estate agents who insist that you have to pay what the sellers want, and at the lenders who disparage the deal.

It **can** be done. But you will only succeed when you crash into the wall of discouragement with sufficient force to break through it. And the wall of discouragement is a part of nearly every real estate deal.

Shark in a feeding frenzy

In my early years, my property acquisition searches always followed the same pattern. I began fairly casually. That got me nowhere. Then, after a month or two, I noticed that I hadn't made much progress. So I stepped up my efforts.

But it still wasn't enough. No acquisition. Then I'd start to get mad at myself. I had decided to buy a property. But here it was months later and I had not done it yet.

Then I'd become almost a **full-time** searcher. Instantly making an appointment to inspect any likely buildings I heard were available. Crunching numbers furiously to see whether an offer was warranted. Then making the offer. At that stage, I was pursuing properties the way a shark in a feeding frenzy pursues food. And only then did I acquire a property.

In recent years, I cut out the time-wasting beginning of that process. Now I pick a city, fly there, rent a car and hotel room, and look at properties...all day, every day. In other words, I now go from a standing start to shark-in-a-feeding-frenzy in one motion. And I buy properties.

Unfortunately, many people never figure this out. They try to become real estate investors. But they feel rushed. All the properties they look at are "dogs." All the "good" properties are snapped up before they have time to make an offer.

When a rookie gets slammed hard for the first time in pro football, the veteran who did it usually helps him up with a quiet, "Welcome to the NFL." When I hear people complaining about the trouble they have finding properties, I feel like saying, "Welcome to real estate investing."

You've got six months

If you prepare thoroughly as described above, you should be able to find a suitable property in a week or three. Maybe it'll take longer. But it should not take more than six months at the longest.

If you've been looking that long and haven't bought a property, you're either too fussy or too slow. Slap yourself in the face, and say, "Thanks, I needed that." Then go out and buy a @#*&! property.

You're not an investor until you get your name on a deed. Talking about it doesn't make you an investor. Looking at buildings doesn't make you an investor. You'll become an investor only when you sign papers and checks and receive a deed.

No warm-ups

Many investors think you should go to an area and scope it out before you make your actual acquisition trip. Nah. Just make the acquisition trip.

Do your homework by reading all the pertinent studies and reports on the area **before** you go there. But do not go there until you're ready to buy. No dry runs. It's an almost total waste of time.

Keep some sort of record of who you talked to and what was discussed. That's to avoid covering the same ground twice. And you want to avoid negotiating on the same property with two different real estate agents.

I accidently got into that position on one property I looked at but didn't buy. And the first agent swore he'd sue me if I bought it and he didn't get a commission. His efforts were so minimal that I don't think he'd have had a prayer of winning. But I had to insist that the second agent indemnify me against the commission claim of the first agent in my purchase agreement. That's a complication you don't need.

Emotional roller coaster

> **Warning**
> During your acquisition effort
> you will ride an emotional roller coaster.

Riding high on Monday; shot down on Tuesday. Your spirits will soar when you find a good-looking building. Then they'll plummet when you hear the seller's ridiculous terms.

The reasons for the soaring and plummeting spirits vary from deal to deal. But the soaring and plummeting itself is standard. Don't let it get you down. It's normal.

Daily routine

Here's the general routine you'll probably find most efficient during your search:

- First thing in the morning: Buy newspapers which cover your area of interest and read classified sections.
- Respond **immediately** to promising ads.
- Call all real estate agents to ask if they have anything.

Of course, when you learn of a possible acquisition, make an appointment **immediately** to inspect it.

When you return to your hotel room, get your messages and return phone calls **immediately**.

I recommend that you have a **cellular phone** and a **computer** when you are in a search mode. The cellular phone will reduce the possibility that you will miss any calls and enable you to respond more quickly. I suspect you can rent a cellular phone if you are investing absentee.

The computer will enable you to evaluate prospective acquisitions more quickly and thoroughly. A laptop is probably best although a desktop computer in your hotel room or home or office would be adequate.

Investors are always asking me what real estate computer software I use, like, or recommend. The answer is **none**. I use, like, and recommend Microsoft Excel and Macintax. Excel is just a spreadsheet program. Macintax is an income tax preparation program. A poll of subscribers of my *Real Estate Investor's Monthly* on the subject found enthusiasm for only one program that I was **not** using. That one was Quicken, a check-writing program. No real estate programs *per se* were mentioned by more than one subscriber.

Don't do anything complicated with the computer. Just use the spreadsheet to calculate the first-year income and expenses, the total square footage, the cap rate, the cash flow, and such. Use the Macintax program to calculate the tax effects of the purchase. (They are now too complicated to arrive at by multiplying tax bracket by depreciation deductions as we did before the Tax Reform Act of 1986.)

Buyer's brokers

Ever since I got into the real estate business in 1969, I've been hearing that buyer's brokers are the latest thing and they'll soon be taking over the business. They've never taken over the business. But they've have become more common.

The line is that most brokers are legally the **agent of the seller**. Therefore, no one's looking out for the **buyer**. The solution, we're told, is a buyer's broker who is the agent of the **buyer** instead of the seller. Instead of signing a listing agreement with a broker, the buyer signs a buyer's broker agreement in which he agrees to pay that broker a commission if he buys a property during a certain period.

I can see how this helps the **broker**. He doesn't have to risk driving someone around in his car showing them properties only to find that they bought through **another** broker leaving them with no commission at all.

But I don't see how it does much for the **buyer**. As a practical matter, there is typically a buyer's broker and a seller's broker in normal real estate deals even though both brokers are technically the seller's agent. In fact, the agent who gets the offer from the buyer watches out for the buyer's interest because he hopes to get the listing when that buyer decides to sell that property or other property in the future.

For the most part, agents look out for **themselves**. Their paramount interest is getting the commission on this deal. So they will only look out for the buyer's or seller's interest to the extent that it does not jeopardize their commission. For example, it's common for agents who find out that both parties want out of the deal to conceal that fact from them thereby leaving them to believe that they are bound to go through with the deal.

The problem is not the seller's agency tradition; it's the commission. The only way you're going to get someone to **really** look out for your interests is to pay him an **hourly fee**. If he gets a commission, whether it be from the seller or the buyer, his overwhelming motivation is to see that the deal **closes** with the **minimum effort** on his part.

Attorneys get paid an hourly fee to look after your interest. And that's fine as far as it goes. But attorneys, in my experience, are typically a little light on practical knowledge of real estate closings. So it would be nice if an experienced real estate agent would consult for you on a fee basis.

Unfortunately, there could be several problems. One is that agents are **deal-oriented**. They hate deal killers and may be loathe to become one even though you are paying them to do precisely that if the deal in question **ought** to be killed.

Another problem is laws against **practicing law without a license**. If an attorney was representing the buyer, I doubt unauthorized practice of law would be a problem. But in a no-attorney deal, it could be.

6

How to Invest Absentee

All things being equal, local investing is better than absentee investing.

All things aren't equal.

If you live in an area which has excellent residential property prospects, by all means invest there. If not, by all means invest elsewhere.

There are efficiencies in being close to your building. Farmers say the best fertilizer is the shadow of the owner. That's also true of real estate to an extent. But if your area is seriously overbuilt...or depressed...or overpriced...the operating losses can easily outweigh the efficiencies of being nearby.

I've been an absentee apartment owner for over fifteen years. And I managed buildings for absentee owners.

Go there

Investing absentee is simple. You fly to the area in question, rent a car and a hotel room, and look at property. As explained elsewhere in the book, I've found it best to prepare by contacting property owners and real estate agents in advance.

I am always exchanging up out of another building when I buy. (For more information on exchanging, see my book *Aggressive Tax Avoidance for Real Estate Investors*.) Tax law requires that an exchangor identify the property he will acquire within 45 days of closing on the old property...and that he close on the new property within 180 days of closing on the old. I point out those deadlines to the Realtors® to convince them that I am a motivated buyer.

One week is all I've ever taken. That requires an uncomfortable amount of haste. But that's life in the real estate business. We almost never have "enough" time or "enough" information when we have to make the decision to go ahead.

In fact, I've found the week in a hotel room to be a necessary motivator and focusing mechanism. When I used to invest locally, I'd take months to find a property. I'd always start rather casually. Then I'd get angry about not having bought a place. Only when I finally got worked up like a shark in a feeding frenzy would I actually buy a property. But shipping myself to Dallas or wherever for a week, I go into my feeding frenzy mode immediately. That saves the months I'd waste if I were investing locally.

Send someone

Some would-be investors protest, "But I can't take off that much time from work (or their medical practice or whatever)." In fact, most people **can** take a week off if they really want to.

If you absolutely, positively can't take the time off, send someone else. It could be your spouse or a partner (although I generally recommend that you avoid any kind of group ownership), or a "hired gun." The typical hired gun would be a real estate agent you trust.

I know a guy who used a real estate agent. The investor is CEO of a large corporation. The investment was personal rather than corporate. He lived in one of the areas where investment property was too expensive. So he decided to buy in the South. He sent a real estate agent. The agent made the acquisition, with the investor flying in at the eleventh hour to meet the seller and see the property. The acquisition performed successfully.

That particular agent told me he would charge $200 per day plus expenses to go from California to Dallas or wherever to locate a property. That was 1982. So figure $400 today. Based on past experience, he said it usually takes about a week to ten days to find a suitable property.

Meet the seller

I recommend that you meet the seller. Most pros feel likewise. You tend to get better terms when you meet face-to-face as a general rule. Real estate agents say the opposite. They believe the parties should **not** meet. Because the principals' egos get involved and explosions are likely.

That's the exception rather than the rule. I think agents fear their contribution will not be appreciated if the principals negotiate without them. And that the chances they'll lose that commission or future commissions from either principal will be increased if they don't "control" the negotiation.

Whenever you use message carriers, "failures to communicate" are likely. We've all seen that party game in which a message is whispered from one person to another. The last person repeats it out loud. Inevitably, it's been unrecognizably garbled. A similar thing can happen and often does when you negotiate through agents.

Communications losses aren't the only problem. It's impossible for you to establish **rapport** and **trust** second hand. And rapport and trust can make all the difference in as emotional an event as a real estate negotiation. In other words, getting face-to-face with the seller usually increases the chances that the deal will go through.

And buyers usually get better terms when they meet the seller face-to-face. There are exceptions, of course. Sometimes the deal will go better if the parties do not meet. Play it by ear. But expect face-to-face to be better in most cases.

Fly in during a contingency period

Real estate deals typically contain an inspection-contingency clause. It says that the terms are such and such but the buyer has seven days or ten days or whatever to inspect the property and/or have it inspected by engineers and such. You can and probably should fly in to inspect a property you had someone else find for you during that contingency period. That could even be done on a weekend if you didn't want to take time off from your normal weekday activity.

Smart sellers resist contingencies. And when they have to accept them, they insist on short fuses. That's fine. You should get enough time to make a decent inspection...a week or two is normal. But you shouldn't waste any negotiating energy getting more than that unless you have some special reason to need extra time.

High-speed, long distance communications

You can and probably should use the various high-speed, long distance communications means available in an absentee acquisition. They include:

- **Overnight couriers** - I generally use Federal Express's Overnight Letter service. It costs under $15 at present.

- **Computer transmission via modem** - Like many real estate investors these days, I have a computer. In fact, this book was written and typeset on one. I also have a modem. That's a device that lets me transmit and receive computer data over the phone. So I can send a contract or other material from my computer to someone else's computer anywhere in the country...as long as that person has a modem, too. The computers need not be compatible. The transmissions are done in ASCII language which is a universal computer code. So if both you and the owner you're buying from have computers and modems, you can use them to facilitate an absentee investment.

- **Fax machine** - If you or the other party does not have one, you can use local store fronts like Mail Boxes, Etc. The companies that provide fax service are listed in the Yellow Pages under "Facsimile Transmission Service."

- **Video teleconferencing** - AT&T and others offer video teleconference service between some major cities. You go to a special conference room in the city in question. And the guys you want to talk to do the same in their city. Then you hold a telephone conversation...except that there are also TV cameras pointing at you...and TV monitors showing the other guy. They also offer facsimile transmission service at the same location. So during the course of your video call, you could also transmit documents back and forth. Video teleconference service is fairly expensive. But so's flying around the country. So it may be cheaper to go by video. Call 800-323-6672 for more information.

Shop-by phone

I believe it's possible to buy a residential building by phone. Not just any building, but a sound, well-selected property. I haven't done it. And have neither the need nor the desire to do so. I only discuss it as part of my effort to rid you of fear of absentee investing.

Here's how I'd invest by phone. First, I'd contact the building owners and real estate brokerage firms in the area in question by letter as before. Only I wouldn't say that I was coming to town. I'd question the callers about the property they wanted to sell me by phone. I'd get a list of the building's tenants either by phone or facsimile or some such. And I'd get the names, addresses, and phone numbers of pertinent people like the property manager, HVAC contractor, and former owner.

I'd call the property manager, HVAC contractor, former owner, and a sample of the tenants and ask them the questions you'll find in the interview section of this book. Then I'd call a building inspection service or engineering firm in the city in question and arrange for them to inspect the property and send me their report by some high-speed transmission method.

If it was a city I was not familiar with, I'd call a bunch of Realtors® from the *Yellow Pages* and ask them where the good and bad neighborhoods were. After talking to several, I'd know pretty much what areas to avoid.

Finally, I'd send a video taping company around to the building. The kind of company that video tapes weddings and personal property inventories. I'd give them a list (like a marked-up copy of this book) of things I wanted to see on the tape. The list would include both the interior and exterior of the building as well as a tour of the neighborhood. In fact, that list would be based on this book. And I'd tell them to Federal Express me the tape.

By the time I got done with all that...especially interviewing the tenants...I suspect my knowledge of that building would equal or exceed that of most buyers who made an on-site inspection. And I could probably do it all within 48 to 72 hours. The main hang-up would probably be the engineering firm. Typically, they'd be busy and would have to schedule their inspection a number of days in advance.

The only thing that would be tough would be an analysis of the overall building appearance and evaluation of the neighborhood. These are difficult to capture even on video tape.

The effectiveness of your pre-purchase evaluation of a property is more a function of the **care** and **thoroughness** you use than the distance between you and the property. A sloppy on-site inspection is **not** superior to a careful, never-set-foot-on-the-place inspection.

Business trip check list

Here's a check list to use when packing to go on or return from a business trip. You will almost certainly need to add items which are unique to you. But this list covers most things.

Business Supplies
- note pad
- mechanical pencil
- business cards
- calculator
- computer
- dictation recorder
- addresses and phone numbers of contacts in the destination city
- Day-Timer calendar
- check book
- telephone answering machine remote beeper
-
-
-

Clothes
- underwear for each day
- socks/hose for each day
- shoes for each event
- pants for each event
- shirts for each event
- ties/scarves
- suits
- belt
- sport coats
- rain coat
- warm coat if cold weather
- gloves if cold weather
- hat
- handkerchiefs
- pajamas
- bathing suit
- athletic clothing and equipment if you plan to work out during trip
- sunglasses
- spare glasses
-
-
-

Miscellaneous
- before leaving, pay bills which will fall due during trip
- books to read on plane
- plane ticket
- wallet
- cash for tips and other items
- travelers cheques
- luggage keys
- street map of distant city
- camera
- prescription medicine you are taking
-
-
-

Toiletries
- razor
- shampoo (now often provided by hotels)
- toothbrush
- dental floss
- toothpaste
- nail clippers
- tweezers
- birth control devices or medicines
- deodorant
- comb/brush
- hair dryer
- contacts cleaner
- make-up/lotions
-
-
-

Business trip expense check list

For tax purposes, you need to keep detailed records of your business expenses. Here's a check list to help you do that. If you have a computer and spreadsheet software, you should create a spreadsheet in this format and type over the old entries each time you go on a business trip.

Date	Meals	Miles	Park	Tips	Tolls	Trans	Misc
MEALS							
Breakfast							
Lunch							
Dinner							
Other refreshments							
TRANSPORTATION							
Home to airport							
Airport parking							
Bridge toll							
Highway toll							
Air fare							
Airport to hotel							
Rental car							
TIPS							
Baggage tip/home airport							
Bag tip/destination airport							
Baggage tip/curb to lobby							
Baggage tip/lobby to room							
MISCELLANEOUS							
Hotel							
Laundry							

PART FOUR:
FINDING A LAWYER

7

How to Find a Good Lawyer
To Handle the Transaction

There are lots of lawyers who would like to handle your apartment-building acquisition. But only a **few** you should use. You want a **specialist**. Unfortunately, there aren't enough apartment building acquisitions for many, or maybe any, lawyers to specialize **that** much. So what you're looking for is a **real estate** attorney. He or she will probably also handle limited partnerships and development matters.

If you are using unusual financing, you may need an attorney who is especially knowledgeable in real estate finance which is a different specialty from real estate closings/limited partnerships/development. And if you are doing an exchange or any other deal in which income taxes are important, you'll need a real estate tax attorney which is a different specialty from both closings/etc. and finance. Finally, you may want to involve an estate planner if you are using a trust or some such. So there are at least four specialties you may need:

- Real estate (closings/limited partnerships/development).
- Real estate finance (mortgages/construction finance/lease-options, etc.)
- Federal income taxation of real estate.
- Estate planner.

This chapter is focused on the first. Although you can find good estate planners and so forth using similar methods.

How to find a top notch attorney

Most of you already have attorneys. And many of you are **not** using the kind of specialist you should. Real estate columnist Robert Bruss, who is an investor and attorney, says a great many general practice attorneys **claim** to be real estate specialists...often with very little experience or training in real estate.

Education and training

As a general rule, the more real estate education and training your adviser has, the better. It can be self taught. Most of **my** real estate is self taught. But some education is necessary.

As far as classroom instruction is concerned, real estate law specialist type information is generally given only in **continuing education** seminars. There are a couple real estate **masters degree** programs around the country. But I suspect the number of real estate attorneys who also have masters degrees in real estate are so few as to be a waste of your time to try to find one in your area.

Local attorney

In my book, *Aggressive Tax Avoidance for Real Estate Investors*, I chastise readers for always wanting a tax attorney who lives in their area. That's because federal tax law is essentially the same nationwide and top-notch tax lawyers are too hard to come by to allow you to only look in your area.

With real estate lawyers, it's just the **opposite**. For starters, you need an attorney in the same state as the property because real estate law is **state law**. Secondly, there are many **county** and **municipal** laws like rent control and zoning which can dramatically affect an apartment building, for example. So you need a local attorney who is familiar with those laws and the people who administer them.

Good **real estate** attorneys are far more common than good **real estate tax** attorneys so confining your search to your local area is no great handicap.

What he reads

You can **become** knowledgeable about real estate law by attending a law school. But you won't **stay** knowledgeable unless you continue to up-date your education. In order to do that, competent real estate lawyers must subscribe to pertinent loose-leaf services and periodicals. If you come across a real estate attorney who claims to be qualified but doesn't subscribe to such services or periodicals, ask him how he stays up-to-date on the latest court decisions, laws, rulings, and regulations. If he's got a satisfactory answer, fine. When you're looking for a real estate attorney, the question, "What periodicals do you subscribe to to stay up-to-date?" is a legitimate one.

Seminars

Real estate attorneys attend pertinent seminars and/or teach them. Bar associations sponsor continuing education seminars. Some focus on real estate topics. Independent companies, real estate periodicals, and educational institutions also sponsor seminars on real estate law topics. Here's a list of some of the organizations:

- Local, state, and national bar associations
- The Practising Law Institute
- American Law Institute
- The Real Estate Institute, NYU
- Realtors® National Marketing Institute
- The Wharton School, Executive Education
- Northwestern Center for Professional Education

Other companies, organizations, and institutions give seminars. To find them, you'll just have to keep your eyes and ears open. If you're on any real estate mailing lists, you'll probably receive announcements of seminars in your area. Make note of who's teaching even if you don't plan to go. And when interviewing a prospective adviser, ask which real estate seminars he's attended or taught recently.

Experience and track record

There's more to real estate law than book-learning. Your adviser should also have experience. Experience as a real estate investor would be desirable. So would experience negotiating with state and local apartment building regulators. In the case of attorneys, trial and appeals court experience could be useful.

Rapport

The more rapport you have with your attorney, the better. Unfortunately, rapport is the **only** selection criteria used by most people. That's the attorney's "bedside manner." Rapport **is** important. But **not** so important that it should be your only criterion.

Service

Your real estate attorney ought to provide good service. That means he meets reasonable deadlines, returns phone calls promptly, doesn't reuse documents from other deals with inappropriate parts left in, doesn't hand you off to an unqualified junior associate, and so forth.

Some professionals...particularly some attorneys, give lousy service. Lousy service is lousy service...whether it's the corner gas station or your real estate attorney. For reasons unknown to me, people who would never tolerate lousy service from the gas station will put up with it for years from their attorney. If your attorney gives lousy service, get rid of him or her.

Sometimes, the most renowned real estate lawyers are **not** the ones you should use. That's because they are the ones most likely to treat clients like dirt. So if I left you with the impression that the most famous guy is the one to get, let me add a warning. Lousy service is often directly proportional to fame. The **second** tier...real estate attorneys who aren't yet big names, may offer the best combination of competence and service.

Integrity

Your tax adviser ought to be honest. For two reasons:

1. Everybody ought to be honest because it's the only moral course.
2. Dishonest attorneys repel people who know them.

It's hard enough to acquire a good investment without having to have the handicap of using an attorney whose name makes sellers reject your offer to avoid dealing with your attorney.

Diligence

Laziness can cost you money. So you want an attorney who does the necessary weekly homework to keep up-to-date. You want one who will dig for ways to structure deals to your advantage. And, when you fight, you want an attorney who will dig for the evidence and authority (court decisions, statutes, etc.) you need to win.

Interest in your problems

By "interest in your problems" I don't mean you should find a bleeding heart. Rather I mean watch out for an attorney who is bored with mundane real estate matters. This, like bad service, is a characteristic common among big names. They've done mundane things a thousand times. Now they want to be "creative."

Beware of such attorneys trying to get you to do "creative" deals which are unnecessary. There are times when "creativity" is exactly what you need. But all things being equal, mundane is far better than "creative" when it comes to legal disputes. So don't let any attorney talk you into "creativity" for "creativity's" sake. Make him explain why you can't do the deal the mundane way before you go "creative." And if he isn't persuasive, and you can't convince him to help you do it the mundane way, get rid of him.

Should you ask your friends?

The main way people find attorneys is to ask their friends. Is that valid? Probably not.

Your friends probably are not real estate law experts. So they aren't qualified to tell who is. But they're not likely to say so. Rather they **will** recommend someone. How do they decide on whom to recommend? Bedside manner.

Another thing you have to guard against is your **being used to return a favor** or earn points with an attorney.

Real estate-agents ought to know the names of local real estate attorneys. Especially if the agent specializes in **apartment buildings**. But real estate agents often get referrals and other favors from attorneys. As a result, they may send you to a guy to whom they owe a favor, or a guy who they want to owe **them** a favor, rather than to the **best** guy. Of course, real estate agents aren't the only ones who might use you to return a favor or earn points with some attorney.

Your friends can help, however, if they know real estate and you trust them to make a recommendation with **your** interest at heart rather than their own.

Teachers and speakers

One of the best ways to spot a top real estate attorney is to see his or her name listed as a teacher of a course or seminar on the subject. I often keep direct-mail brochures I receive on real estate seminars. One reason is they provide a file of the names of interesting real estate people. Among the brochures are many on legal topics. And in virtually every case, the name and other details about the instructor are listed.

Trade conventions, both state and national, typically have a number of seminars. Sometimes, at real estate conventions, they offer a seminar or talk on a real estate legal topic. There's typically one or two speakers or a panel of three to six people. The subject of the talk, and the names of the speakers/panelists are listed in the convention program. These are typically leaders in the field.

You can get information on such convention seminars and their speakers from the sponsoring trade association. There's a list of real estate trade associations in the back of the book.

Trade association committees

Trade associations also have standing committees. For example, the American Bar Association (ABA) has a "Section" devoted to "Real Property, Probate, and Trust Law." Under that "Section" are subgroups devoted to:

- Conveyancing
- Environmental law
- State and local taxation
- Real estate investment and so forth.

The members of these committees are listed in the ABA's *Directory*. In each subgroup, a Chairman, Vice-Chairman, and often other names are listed. Presumably, these are ABA members with particular interest and expertise in these subjects. The phone numbers and addresses of these individuals are listed in the back of the *Directory*. Most trade associations have similar committees and directories in one form or another. You can generally get the directory or the information from it from the trade-association office.

Book authors

Top notch real estate lawyers often write books on the subject. So it may be worth your while to contact real estate law book authors.

I'm not in the advice business other than through my writing. Most real estate law book authors **are** in the advice business, however. Or they know someone who is.

Where do you find the names of real estate book authors? The "Pertinent References" appendix at the back of this book is a good place to start. You can also check the *Subject Guide to Books in Print*. It's published by R.R. Bowker and is available in most libraries. The Real Estate Publishing Company (PO Box 41177, Sacramento, CA 95841) publishes *Real Estate Books in Print*.

How do you track down the author after you've found his name? Usually, the information in the "about the author" section will tell you enough. If not, you can write to him in care of the publisher. Or you might be able to track him down through *Who's Who* or *Contemporary Authors*. Both are typically in libraries. You can usually get the information over the phone by calling the library reference desk.

Before I leave books, don't overlook the "Acknowledgments" section in most real estate law books. There the author thanks people who helped him write the book. One of the tax attorneys I've used was listed in the acknowledgment section of a book on exchanging. So, if not the author, then perhaps one of the people who helped him will help you.

Don't assume a "big author" would never talk to little ol' you. Take it from me, book authors are "real people." Writing books is a job like any other job. The typical book author is a one or two person operation (author and spouse or assistant). Unless he's frantically running around doing talk shows (not likely in real estate law) or making speeches (more likely), he'll probably be pretty accessible. If he's got sense, he'll realize it's good to talk to his readers...if only for market-research purposes.

Article authors

Book authors aren't the only writers of interest. Article authors may be an even better source. Certainly there are more articles written each year than books. So you have more people to choose from. Although a book is better evidence of legal expertise than an article.

You can usually get the address of the author by getting a copy of the article. Typically, there's a little blurb saying, "The author is a partner in the Kansas City law firm of O'Malley, Weinstein, and Wong." From there, it's just a simple matter of calling the information operator in Kansas City. If that information's not in the article, call the periodical.

Attorney in prominent court cases

In some real estate court cases, the person acted as his own attorney. But in most, he had an attorney. And his attorney's name is usually listed in the decision.

The attorney may not have been a top notch expert on the issue in the case **before** it started. But I'll bet he is now. In the process of preparing for a trial, any attorney worth his salt will thoroughly study the law on the item in dispute. By the time he's **done**, he **is** an expert on it.

That's true win or lose. In the first two editions of this book, I cited "winners of landmark cases" as attorneys to contact. I now say winners **or** losers. Unless a reading of the case reveals that it was lost through poor preparation on the part of the attorney. But losing doesn't prove the attorney is bad. The client may have presented him with an impossible situation. And there's no reason to restrict the category to "landmark" cases. All you really need is an attorney who fought a case like yours recently.

The attorney's name is usually printed on the first page of the court decision. Sometimes, only the name is listed. Other times; the name, law firm, and city. When only the name is given, you can often figure out the rest from the location of the court. Or, with just his name, you can look him up in Martindale-Hubbell's directory of attorneys. Or you could simply call the court and ask. They'll usually tell you. I've called the U.S. Supreme Court for similar information. A perfectly normal secretary comes on the line and tells you what you want...even there. There is not, as you might expect, a thundering, deep-voiced judge demanding to know, "How dare you call the United States Supreme Court!?"

Editors of trade journals

Editors of trade journals rarely are practicing legal advisers. But they probably know someone who is.

I once needed an attorney to help me negotiate with a major book publisher. So I called the editor of *Writer's Digest* magazine. He gave me the number of one of the best writer's attorneys in the nation. I called her and she represented me in the contract negotiations.

This suggestion does **not** apply to trade journals published by bar associations. They'll tell you that **all** their members are qualified. Baloney.

Trade journals which accept advertising will probably steer you toward their advertisers if they have any who are real estate lawyers. Newsletter editors, of which I am one, have neither advertisers nor members to please. So they can give you objective advice.

Beware of big firms

John Beck is an Alameda, California attorney/real estate investor. He used to work for a big-name accounting firm. He remembers a meeting held to see how they could discourage "little guys" from being clients. They only wanted corporations and large companies.

So before you trot off to a big-name law firm, consider that they may be holding meetings on how to get **rid** of people like you. One of the ways they probably come up with is **charging you more** than they charge the clients they **want**.

Special certifications and designations

Some organizations give certifications and designations which are indicators of real estate law competence.

Certified Commercial Real Estate Specialist: This is a certification given by a Texas board of legal specialization. As you would expect, it applies primarily to Texas attorneys. Such boards will generally send you a copy of their roster of specialists. You can generally tell if your state has such certifications by looking in the Attorney section of the Yellow Pages of a large city in your state. Many of the attorneys who have such certifications will brag about it in their ads. If no attorney mentions such a certification, your state probably does not have such a certification program.

Certified Commercial-Investment Member (CCIM) of the Realtors® National Marketing Institute (RNMI): This is a designation given out by a National Association of Realtors® subsidiary. To get it, you have to graduate from a number of courses and be approved as well on the basis of your commercial-investment experience. A number of CCIMs are also attorneys. You can get a directory of the CCIMs in your area from the Commercial-Investment Division of the RNMI.

No credential is sufficient

Does the fact that someone teaches or writes about taxes, or holds a certification, guarantee that he's the right adviser?

No.

A Texas attorney who is a Certified Commercial Real Estate Specialist represented a guy I was in a dispute with in 1988. We agreed to settle the dispute. Part of the agreement called for me to assign my insurance policy to the other guy in a transaction where I was deeding an apartment building to him.

I drew up an agreement with appropriate wording. The attorney **ignored** my agreement and drew up his own from scratch. He not only **left out** my clause obligating me to assign the insurance, he **added** a clause saying all verbal agreements were hereby declared null and void.

Since I thought I had been jerked around unfairly in the deal…jerking around which cost me over $2,000 in legal fees…I took advantage of the opportunity created by the lawyer's version to **cancel** the insurance policy in question rather than assign it to the new owner. That got me a refund in the neighborhood of $2,000…and cost my opponent that much extra for a new policy.

Making sure you have the building insured when you acquire it is pretty basic. Incorporating all the clauses in a pre-existing version of an agreement when you draw up a new version is also pretty basic. So here's a case where having a high-falutin' certification was not a guarantee against incompetence.

Does the fact that someone does **not** teach or write about taxes, or hold a certification, prove that he's **un**qualified?

No.

Then why seek someone with such credentials?

First, teaching, writing, and being listed in a directory of specialists makes an adviser visible to us on the outside. In other words, they are ways of separating real estate law specialists from the mass of attorneys.

Second, the fact that someone writes, teaches, or holds a certification is **some** evidence, albeit imperfect, of competence in the field.

Finally, separating the real estate law specialists from the rest of attorneys is not the entire selection process.

How to interview a prospective tax adviser

In the material above, I did not mean to say that as soon as you find someone who wrote a real estate law article you say, "Great! You're hired." At that stage, you've found a **candidate**, not an adviser. Don't make the hire-or-not decision until after you've asked him a few questions.

A quality real estate lawyer won't mind questions about his qualifications

When I first proposed the questions below in my tax seminar, I was concerned that top professionals might be offended by them. So I advised my students to ask them tactfully. But all of my seminar audiences included some tax professionals. And they said they'd **like** prospective clients to ask these kinds of questions. The reason is that they've spent years becoming a specialist and they'd love a chance to brag about it. In his book, *How to Win Friends and Influence People* Dale Carnegie pointed out that everyone likes to talk about themselves and their accomplishments. In asking these questions, you're giving the prospective real estate lawyer the chance to do just that.

There are two kinds of real estate lawyers who will balk at answering these questions. The first group is made up of attorneys who are more embarrassed about the **answers** than they are angry at the **questions**. But they'll likely react belligerently to the questions to cover up their lack of qualifications.

The second group is made up of real estate lawyers who have become convinced that they are universally known. They believe they are so famous that **everyone already knows** their qualifications. I've got news for them, and you. There is **no** real estate lawyer in the country who is so well known that there aren't many smart, successful real estate investors who have never heard of him. And you don't want to work with the guys who **think** they're universally known anyway. They're so full of themselves they often give lousy service.

Competent real estate lawyers who possess accurate self-images and human-size egos will be glad to answer these questions. If the guy you're considering balks, find someone else.

Real estate lawyer interview questions

• What year did you start your real estate law career? _____

• Did you ever work for the state department of real estate (or whatever it's called in your state)? In what capacity? How long? _____
_____

• Did you ever work for any other real estate agency or company? _____
_____

• Roughly, how many times have you represented real estate investors in real estate legal disputes? What's your batting average? _____
_____

• Roughly how many times have you fought real estate cases in court? Batting average? _____

• What legal/accounting/real estate degrees do you have? From what institutions?
_____
_____

• What other real estate training do you have? _____
_____
_____

• Do you have any real estate certifications or designations? _____
_____
_____

• Have you attended continuing education courses or seminars pertinent to my problem (whatever you're going to the adviser for)? _____
_____

• Have you taught real estate courses pertinent to my problem? _____

_____

• What periodicals or real estate services pertinent to real estate law do you subscribe

  to? _____

• What is your fee? _____

• Do you have expertise in real estate finance? If so, how did you acquire it?

_____

_____

• Ask about a recent real estate law development. _____

_____

• Have you written any articles or books on the subject of real estate law? _____

_____

_____

• Have you made any speeches or taught any courses on real estate law? _____

_____

• References: _____

_____

_____

 Professionals like attorneys and accountants may **not** give out the names of their clients without the client's permission. Obtaining that permission is time-consuming and a bit embarrassing to the adviser and it's a bother to the client to answer questions from some stranger. So I wouldn't ask a tax adviser for references on a transaction in which his fee is likely to be less than $2,500. If you're unhappy with him, you can just get rid of him. But if his fee is likely to be <u>more</u> than $2,500, and the involvement is such that it would be difficult to change advisers, ask for the names of clients he has worked with on similar problems. Examples would include hiring a lawyer for a long, drawn out real estate transaction in which it would be costly to have to train a new adviser midstream.

Ask about a recent real estate law development

A good tax adviser is up-to-date. Every couple of months, an important court decision, ruling, regulation, or new law pertaining to real estate comes out. Your adviser should be aware of it. To test him, look up recent developments in a periodical which covers real estate law in your state. For example, in California, *The Robert Bruss California Real Estate Law Newsletter* covers recent court decisions. The lawyer need not subscribe to a **particular** publication. But if he really is a real estate lawyer, he will subscribe to **some** publication which would have brought recent state court decisions to his attention. Find a recent issue of your state's publications. Make mental note of the details of a couple such recent decisions and ask the prospective attorney about them.

Be careful about this test, though. If you pick an unimportant, obscure decision, it's not a meaningful test. And give the guy enough slack to miss an item occasionally due to vacation or whatever.

One real estate lawyer told me he thought this test was too tough. I disagree. I could pass it. And I'm not an attorney who gives advice on a daily basis. For example, this year there was a California decision which said mobilehome park rent control must contain an interim decontrol provision. If you asked me about that, I'd remember its main points. If you wanted more details, I'd have to look it up.

Questions to ask other clients

If you do get references from the lawyer in question, here are some questions to ask them:

• Do you recommend (name of attorney)? _____

• Did he return your phone calls reasonably promptly? _____

• Did he meet reasonable deadlines? _____

• Do you feel you were overcharged? _____

• Were documents carefully prepared (rather than copied from other deals with inappropriate parts left in)? _____

• Were you shunted off to a junior associate? _____

• Did he seem to know real estate law well? _____

• Do you plan to use this attorney again? If not, why not? _____

_____

The proof is in the pudding

After you've interviewed the prospective attorney, (and where necessary, one or two of his clients) you should have a pretty solid basis for hiring him or not. But the **final** proof is in the pudding. How do you like working with him? How competent does he seem to be? Is he earning his fee? If there was a dispute, did he argue your case effectively?

I only use real estate lawyers on an *ad hoc* basis. I do not have anyone on retainer. I recommend you do likewise…unless you do deals on a monthly or weekly basis. If you just use the attorney every now and then, he'll hardly notice if you "fire" him by not using him again. But a retainer requires an actual firing which is unpleasant and traumatic. As a result, many investors can't bear to do the necessary firing so they continue to use, and pay, an attorney they're unhappy with.

Your arrangement with the adviser about his fee

Quality real estate legal advice is usually expensive. Top-notch real estate attorneys charge well over $100 an hour.

Many laymen are intimidated by accountants, attorneys, and other professionals. Often, they're reluctant to bring up fees because they think doing so will make them look "small time." "Big time" investors, they imagine, never discuss fees. As in, "If you need to ask 'how much,' you can't afford me."

The Bar Association Code says discuss fees up front

The American Bar Association has a Model Code of Professional Responsibility…a sort of code of ethics. Regarding fees, it says,

> *Ethical Consideration 2-19: As soon as feasible after a lawyer has been employed, it is desirable that he reach a clear agreement with his client as to the basis of the fee charges to be made. Such a course will not only prevent later misunderstanding but will also work for good client relations between the lawyer and the client. It is usually beneficial to reduce to writing the understanding of the parties regarding the fee, particularly when it is contingent. A lawyer should be mindful that many persons who desire to employ him may have had little or no experience with fee charges of lawyers, and for this reason he should explain fully to such persons the reasons for the particular fee arrangement he proposes.*

That is terrible writing which I can't let pass without translating it into readable English. Here's what they are trying to say:

> *You should agree on the fee with your client as soon as possible. That will prevent misunderstandings and make for good relations. It's usually wise to put the fee agreement in writing, especially when it's contingent. And don't forget that many clients have little or no experience with lawyers. You should be especially careful to give those people a complete explanation of how the fee will be calculated.*

Only a fool fails to discuss the fee

Regarding the notion that "big time" investors never discuss the fee, forget it. To paraphrase a line from an old Midas Muffler commercial, "How do you think big time guys got to **be** big time guys?" Not by giving blank checks to their lawyers.

A good businessman controls his costs. To not do so is to risk becoming a **former** businessman. Professional fees for legal advice are no exception. I have seen many legal advice clients get hit with much bigger bills than they expected. In almost every case, that surprise can be traced to the same source...failure to agree on the fee at the outset.

Bring it up at the beginning...and put it in writing

I've worked with a number of real estate attorneys and accountants. Rarely have **they** mentioned the fee up front...as urged by the Code of Professional Responsibility. That being the case, **you** initiate the fee discussion.

Here's how the discussion between you and the attorney should go:

Investor: "Bob, I want to exchange out of my Springfield property. I'll need you to check the listing agreement and exchange agreement. And I might need you for other things that come up. What will you charge?"

Adviser: *"Well, a lot of things can come up, Jack, so I can't give a fixed price. If I did, I'd have to pad it to protect myself. My hourly rate is $150."*

Investor: "OK. For now, all I need you to do is look over the listing agreement to make sure there's nothing in it that would jeopardize the exchange. Think you can do that in less than an hour?"

Adviser: *"Probably."*

Investor: "Fine, here it is. I'd like to have it back Tuesday. Is that a problem?"

Adviser: *"No."*

Investor: "I figure it'll take an hour or less. If it looks like it's going to run over an hour, Bob, please call me before you continue. OK?"

Adviser: *"Will do."*

As soon as you get back to your office, send the adviser a note restating the agreement: "$150 an hour. Call before going over an hour."

Time and materials

Most real estate investors know that you should not deal with subcontractors on a "time and materials" basis. But they **will** accept it when dealing with a lawyer.

That's probably necessary because most attorneys and accountants insist on doing business that way. But that doesn't mean you have to give the adviser a blank check. Set a **limit**.

Warning: Some attorneys will agree to the limit, then **ignore** it. That happened to me a couple months ago with a bill for a will.

Refuse to pay the bill. Send them the agreed amount and a copy of the agreement. I had to do that with a publishing attorney once. She apologized and adjusted the bill down to the agreed amount.

> **NOTE:**
> Setting a limit on attorney fees is one of the most important points in this book.

Insist on an itemized bill

Do not tolerate bills that say merely, "For services rendered: $604." Barry Gallagher's book *How to Hire a Lawyer* has an excellent chapter on what a legal bill should look like...including a sample of a properly detailed bill.

Additional notes on finding a lawyer:

PART FIVE:
<u>THE PHYSICAL INSPECTION</u>

8

Environmental Audit

Welcome to the '90s. In the '80s and before, investors bought real estate without getting an environmental audit done. No more.

If you don't insist on one, the lender will. And in this day and age, investors or lenders who do **not** insist on an environmental audit need their heads examined.

Scope of the problem

You probably think the savings and loan problem is big. And it is. But the environmental liability problem is even bigger.

- A survey of members of the Mortgage Bankers Association revealed that about 20% of all real properties have environmental problems.

- Underground tank specialist Joyce Rizzo says clean up costs for leaking tanks can exceed $500,000.

- A Seattle area owner of a $750,000 apartment building listed it for sale. The buyer demanded an environmental audit. The audit found asbestos and soil contaminated by petroleum. Clean-up cost: $450,000. Since the mortgage on the property was $500,000, the revelation of the audit is that the owner has not the $250,000 equity he thought he had. Rather he has **minus** $200,000 equity. And you are **personally liable** for the cleanup cost regardless of whether you are personally liable for the mortgage.

• A Jasper, FL couple found that their house had asbestos in the walls and ceilings. The cost to remove it exceeds what the house would be worth without any asbestos. It can't be sold or rented. No contractor has been willing to tear it down because demolition of such a building requires expensive procedures similar to removing only the asbestos.

• It cost $11.6 million to clean up one house in Lansdowne, PA. A previous owner had assembled radium needles in the basement in the '50s.

• Five homes in Macomb Township, MI had their assessed values cut to $100 because of ground water contamination from a nearby dump. A home across from the dump had sold for $199,000 not long before the contamination was discovered.

• Michigan Bankers Association consultant Jud Moran says, "It's very easy to do a million dollars worth of damage to a $100,000 property. Tom Durham of Swanson Environmental, Inc. in Farmington, MI says, "It is real easy to get up to a half million in clean-up cost."

Enough said on the scope of the problem.

How to avoid contaminated properties

The short answer to avoiding contaminated properties is you have an environmental audit done. To date, the real estate business has treated environmental liability risk as the equivalent of termite risk or title-flaw risk. You just open the *Yellow Pages* and call a termite inspector or a title insurance company or an environmental auditor and he takes care of the problem. Not so fast. Environmental liability ain't termites or an overlooked water bill.

As stated above, the stakes in environmental liability are extremely high. Overlooked termite damage may cost you $3,000 or $10,000. But overlooked contaminants can cost you your life's savings.

Secondly, environmental liability is an extremely **fast-changing** area of law and science and mass hysteria. Termite damage can be detected by standard inspection procedures and the repair cost is both relatively low and highly predictable once the damage has been discovered. Title documents are recorded according to standard procedures in the county court house and title flaws have been litigated in the courts for hundreds of years, thereby establishing clear search and risk parameters upon which title insurance companies can base premiums.

But with toxics, we don't know where we stand. From near zero (lead paint) in the early '80s, the list of toxics building owners worry about has now grown to a dozen or more (asbestos, hexavelent chromium, petroleum, radon, etc.). We don't know what new toxics will be added to the list in future years.

The legislatures have only recently begun to pass **new laws** about disclosure and clean up of toxics. Many more such laws are now being proposed. The **courts** are just beginning to interpret those laws. And their decisions have been distressingly expansive. So even environmental lawyers don't know what the law is now, let alone what it will be during the time you own a building you buy today.

Science marches on...one day adding a substance previously thought harmless to the list of toxics...another day announcing that a substance previously identified as toxic really isn't. That march of science can be devastating to your real estate investment. And it is totally unpredictable.

Then there's the **hysteria**. In spite of scientific evidence to the contrary, large segments of the public are hysterically afraid of such things as Agent Orange, Malathion, non-Dalkon Shield intrauterine birth control devices, cyclamates, fluoride, asbestos-containing building materials already installed in buildings, Alar, DPT vaccine, "sick-building syndrome" where neither human nose nor scientific instruments can detect any unusual odors or gases, many agricultural pesticides and food additives. When they first began to be used, people were afraid of electric lights and microwave ovens.

While it can be proven that these substances are either harmless or that they make sense because they prevent worse harms, that has not saved the owners of such substances from losing millions in the form of court judgments or lost business due to being shunned by the public.

So in short, an environmental audit, even a thorough one, leaves you far short of confident that you will not lose money due to environmental problems in the property you are buying. Having said that, I'll proceed with how to get the audit performed.

Phased audits

In order to hold down the high costs of environmental audits, the standard industry practice is to do the audits in phases. Phase Ia involves:

- Review of government records looking for indications of contamination on the property in question (one firm charges $95 and up to perform this check for a house and $295 and up for commercial properties).
- Forty-year title search to see what kind of uses occurred on the property in the past.
- Interview with current owner.

Some people believe that if there are no indications of contamination in the Phase Ia audit, you assume the property's clean. I, and others, disagree. We believe Phase Ia and Ib are the minimum. Phase Ib involves a walk-through inspection by an engineer. Phase Ib is expensive: about $1,500 to $3,000 according to Mark Bennett, an executive with an environmental firm in Michigan.

If the Phase Ib audit reveals any suspicious items, you have to proceed to Phase II. Phase II involves taking samples of the suspect materials, soil, water, or air and having them tested at a laboratory. Fees for such tests start at $2,000 typically. Although verification of asbestos can be obtained for about $50 per sample.

Swanson Environmental charges $2,000 to $4,000 for "initial studies" of a property, $3,000 to $6,000 to study "hot spots," and $5,000 to $20,000 to determine the extent of contamination. Joyce Rizzo, president of Lexicon Environmental Associates, Inc. (215-344-3380) in West Chester, PA puts the cost of a Phase Ib audit at $2,000 to $5,000.

Who pays?

Normally, the prospective purchaser of the property pays for the inspections which he requires. But those inspections generally cost relatively little...and the seller generally agrees to fix or credit the buyer for whatever the inspectors find.

With environmental audits, however, the cost is not little. It's quite high. Furthermore, the cost of cleaning up what the auditor finds is often astronomical, so much so that the seller refuses to either clean the property up or credit the buyer the clean-up cost at closing.

So a buyer who paid thousands of dollars for an environmental audit can find himself with nothing but a dead deal for his expense. Buyers who put themselves in a position where that can happen are nuts.

On the other hand, sellers hate the very idea of an environmental auditor even setting foot on their property, let alone paying for it. When you say you want an environmental audit, they often throw tantrums in which they claim that all this concern about asbestos and such is foolish hysteria (largely true) and that by wanting an audit, you are part of the hysteria. While it is true that most of the environmental clean ups required of owners are unnecessary wastes of money, those clean ups are an inescapable fact of life in the '90s. You must **not** let the seller or real estate agent talk you out of having an environmental audit performed.

It seems to me that you should pick the auditor and the seller should pay for the audit. If the deal falls through as a result of the seller refusing to clean up contamination found by the audit, the **seller** should get stuck with the bill. If the audit shows a **clean** bill of health, the **buyer** should pay for it. Who pays in the event there is **some** contamination but the deal **goes through** should be a matter for negotiation. Clearly, existing contamination is the seller's responsibility. So he should pay for the **finding** of it as well as the clean up. If the deal does not go through, the seller can at least use the audit in future efforts to clean up, finance, or sell the property. The audit is useless to a prospective buyer on a dead deal. On the other hand, the seller who owns a clean property should **not** have to pay for the buyer's environmental nervousness if the property is clean.

At present, sophisticated buyers and lenders always require environmental audits. Only unsophisticated buyers of small units and home buyers are doing without environmental audits. They are crazy.

In the not-too-distant future, **all** buyers and lenders will require them. That means buying with**out** one now will give you the worst of all worlds: you'll overlook any contamination on your property now but it will be found in a few years when you try to sell or refinance.

Environmental auditors

A high-school dropout may be perfectly acceptable to do a termite inspection of your property. But **not** an environmental audit. With the stakes as high as they are, and the subject matter as complicated as it is, you need an **engineer** to perform an environmental audit. An environmental engineer.

The National Association of Environmental Risk Auditors started in 1988. They award three designations:

- Certified Environmental Risk Screener
- Certified Environmental Audit Reviewer
- Certified Environmental Risk Auditor

For its highest designation, the Certified Environmental Risk Auditor, the National Association of Environmental Risk Auditors requires formal education in:

- Civil engineering or
- Life sciences or
- Hard sciences or
- Law,

plus nine days of courses including on-site training. They also have a **continuing education** requirement for their designees because of the changing science in the field. States will probably soon start licensing environmental auditors.

Pollution Engineering magazine (708-635-8800) publishes an annual directory. A listing there is not proof of competence, but it is a useful starting point. For referrals, ask:

- Environmental lawyers.
- Lending institutions.
- State agencies which regulate toxics.

Of course, the *Yellow Pages* covers this subject under "Environmental & Ecological Services."

Data bases

Because checking public records is now a standard part of the Phase I audit, companies have sprung up offering computer data bases of public records relating to contamination. TOXICHECK covers such records in the state of Michigan and is provided by Environmental Information Services (313-647-5408).

Vista Environmental runs a **national** data base.

Not total protection

Title insurance gives you more or less total protection from risk of loss due to title problems. Termite guarantees give you more or less total protection from termite damage. A roof inspection by a competent roofer gives you almost total protection from roof repair surprises. But environmental audits give nowhere near the protection of these other common pre-purchase inspections.

You could have the building you plan to buy certified clean by the world's best environmental auditor, then lose your life's savings to environmental liability on the property. How?

- The auditor fails to perform a procedure which is later determined to be part of the minimum needed to satisfy the "all appropriate inquiry" standard of the CERCLA.

- The property is found to be contaminated with a substance which was not considered a hazard when you bought the building.

- The public develops a hysterical fear of a substance which scientists say is safe, but which is in your building.

- A new law is passed in the future which requires ruinously expensive removal of a substance not now required to be removed.

- The auditor is unable to inspect nearby properties, thereby overlooking some contamination which renders all properties in the neighborhood worthless.

- Two guys pull up at 2:00 a.m. and dump 20 fifty-five gallon drums of toxic chemicals on the back of your property.

- New, tougher standards lower the acceptable level of toxic substances and put your property into an unacceptable category.

Environmental law and science are young and constantly changing. So even an investor who makes a good faith effort to take appropriate care cannot know where he stands on closing day. In short, even the best environmental audit is to environmental liability what a 20-foot-wide dam is to a 40-foot-wide river.

Your contract with the auditor

James Witkin, an environmental lawyer with the Washington, DC law firm of Content, Tatusko, and Patterson, says your contract with the environmental auditor should include the following:

- **Indemnification**. The auditor should indemnify you against losses you suffer as a result of problems with his audit.

- **Insurance**. You should require that the auditor's insurance agent provide you with a certificate proving that he has at least $1,000,000 of errors and omission insurance.

- **Liability**. Do not agree to a cap on the auditor's liability which is less than the amount of his errors and omission insurance coverage.

- **Licensing**. Require the auditor to warrant that he has all necessary licenses and permits and that he will not break any laws in the conduct of his audit.

- **Confidentiality**. Prohibit the auditor from divulging the contents of his audit to anyone but you without your written permission.

- **Deadline**. Put a deadline and time is of the essence clauses in the agreement.

- **Termination**. Make sure you have the right to terminate the contract for good cause and bring in a new auditor.

Home Buyer's Guide...

You can get a 42-page *Home Buyer's Guide to Environmental Hazards* from the Federal National Mortgage Association, Department E, P.O. Box 23867, Baltimore, MD 21203.

9

Structure Inspection

Unless you are an expert in everything from termite damage to roofs, you'll probably want one or more experts in various aspects of building and their equipment to inspect the property and give you a report. And even if you don't care about such an inspection, your lender probably will insist on it.

If your prospective acquisition is small, a house-inspection service is probably adequate for you and your lender. Larger buildings require an engineer *per se*. There's no specific cut-off size that I'm aware of. In general, lenders want engineers when the property has characteristics not normally found in single-family homes...like:

- Flat roofs.
- Parking lots.
- Central heating, air-conditioning, and hot water systems which serve more than one unit.

The Federal Home Loan Mortgage Corporation required me to get an engineer report when I bought a 25-unit apartment building which they financed. That lender directed the engineer to render an opinion on:

- Overall condition of the structure.
- Roof.
- Foundation.

• Heating and air-conditioning systems.

That inspection report was in the form of a letter of a little more than a page. It said the HVAC system is composed of unitary fan units [in each apartment]. No mention of the central compressor, condenser, cooling tower, hot water boiler, or central hot-water heater system.

Cost

My report cost $300 in 1983. An investor I just interviewed got an engineer's report on a house with a foundation and retaining wall problem for $200 in 1989.

"I'm not responsible"

If you're not careful, the report you get will say nothing. That is, it will merely acknowledge that the signer visited the property and saw various parts of it, but that he really doesn't know whether it's a good structure or not. More than anything else, the report says, "I'm not responsible."

The report I got on the 25-unit apartment building said nothing. It used the word "cursory" four times. Their opinion of the roof was that it was "not accessible; therefore no comment can be made."

The report ended with these "I'm not responsible" paragraphs:

The above comments/opinions were developed from a brief tour of existing facilities and a cursory review of the original construction documents; therefore, we at X Associates cannot and will not assume any responsibility or liability involved in the sale and/or purchase of this property.

Additionally, since we were directed to provide a cursory tour of the existing facilities and Construction Documents, we cannot and will not assume any responsibility or liability with respect to the design and construction of this facility.

After these weasel words were embossed two very impressive seals indicating the registered architect and registered engineer status of the cursory inspectors.

These say-nothing reports are most likely when you allow the seller to get the report in question. Never allow the seller to order the report. I don't remember who got this one. I do remember that although the lender accepted it before closing, they belatedly read it afterward and ordered another report at **their** expense.

That report was more thorough (four plus pages and 15 Polaroid photos). It had not a word about the cursoriness of the inspection nor anything about avoiding responsibility or liability. Its conclusion was a model of courage compared to the original report. It said,

It is the opinion of the writers that this apartment complex is in comparable condition to similar units of the same age. All of the above-mentioned deficiencies are repairable, and with proper repair and continued good maintenance this apartment building should have an economic life an additional 30 years.

In other words, the inspectors said this is your basic, average apartment building with no serious problems...which it is and which is all the lender really needed to know.

"It's not brand new"

There's another kind of report. It's not worthless. But it's a lot less helpful than a good report. That's one where the inspector finds fault with everything that's not still under warranty. To such an inspector, a two-year old hot-water heater requires a paragraph of meaningless drivel about the possibility that it could go any time...even though it's in fine shape and hot-water heaters normally last ten years or more. And so on all through the building.

While such information may be accurate and useful when put in perspective, it is hard to make efficient use of a document which simply states the obvious for page after page after page.

How to find a good one

My **mortgage broker** found both the lousy and the good engineers. Indeed, since the engineering report is frequently a lender requirement, selecting an engineer **without** asking the lender to preapprove him or her could be risky. So go to your lender first and ask whose reports they've relied upon and liked in the past.

Even if you aren't getting a new institutional loan, asking a lender or mortgage broker to recommend an engineer is still a good idea. They have the most frequent need for such reports. The typical investor doesn't do enough deals to know who the best engineers are.

Articles in **trade journals** are useful for spotting engineers who specialize in residential property. I found a good roofing engineer to help diagnose and replace a flat roof at one of my buildings. He had written an article on flat roofs in *Texas Apartments*, the magazine of the Texas Apartment Association.

Ask the local **apartment association** to recommend an engineer or refer you to some of their members who might be able to make such a referral. When my insurance was cancelled twice in the space of a month in 1985, I asked the Texas Apartment Association if they could help. They recommended Greg Crouch, an insurance consultant (512-467-7299) in Austin, TX, who not only got me new insurance fast but who actually reduced my premium per dollar of coverage. The insurance consultant was not an engineer *per se*, but he was a similar sort of professional.

Recommendations of people in the apartment management or acquisition business can be useful. I found a top notch foundation engineer by calling an apartment syndicator I knew. Turns out, that foundation engineer had also written a book on the subject. So **book authors** is another source. In the typical case, you won't have the good luck I had to be interested in a foundation of an apartment building in the same metropolitan area as the nation's best foundation engineer. But engineers will generally travel (for an extra fee) to wherever you need them. Or they can usually refer you to a colleague in the area in question. Your local librarian can help you locate the names of the books on engineering subjects pertinent to the building you are considering buying. She or he can also help you track down the author.

If necessary, start with the *Yellow Pages*. The good engineer which my lender hired was listed in the *Yellow Pages* under, "Engineers-Consulting." The bad one was listed under "Architects," for whatever that's worth.

Check the engineer's **license**. Although both the good and bad engineers who inspected my building had licenses.

Ask for **references**…preferably from residential property building buyers like yourself.

Questions to ask the prospective engineer

If you're going to pay an engineer $300 or more, you're entitled to ask him a few questions. To not be able to do so would force you to buy an engineer in a poke. As my experience above indicates, some of them produce worthless or near worthless reports.

• When did you become a licensed engineer? _____

• May I see your resume? _____

• Roughly how many residential buildings have you inspected? _____

• What engineering degrees do you have (if not on resume)? _____

• Do you have errors and omissions insurance? _____

• What would your fee be for this inspection? _____

• Please give me the names of residential building acquisition clients you've done

   inspections for. _____

_____

• May I see a copy of a recent inspection report you did on an apartment or similar

   building? I don't need to know the address of the property or name of the client so

   you can separate or cover that up if you wish. (Look for "I'm-not-responsible" or

   "It's-not-brand new" style reports. _____

Questions to ask other clients of the engineer

• Do you recommend (name of engineer) _____

• Would you use him or her again? _____

• Did he or she make the inspection and produce the report reasonably promptly?

_____

• Did he or she try to charge more than agreed? _____

• Was the report overly long or too brief? _____

Additional notes:

10

What to Take With You

One-stop shopping

It's best to make just one or two inspections. If you have to make more, you antagonize the seller and waste the time of whoever shows you through the property. In addition, if another buyer makes an offer while you're still inspecting, you may lose a good investment.

The key to doing just one inspection is **thoroughness**. Thorough preparation and a thorough inspection when you get there. Part of the preparation is to make sure you have everything you need when you arrive. That's what this check list is about.

In your car trunk

Put the following in your car trunk. You may not need them. And they're too bulky to carry through the building until you're sure you do need them.

- **Binoculars** - To inspect upper walls and pitched roofs without climbing a ladder.

- **Drop light** - To inspect dark areas like basements, storage, crawl spaces. Maybe you'd rather not. But it's too important to skip. A lot of money's at stake, remember?

- **Extension cord**.

- **Socket-to-plug adaptor** - Often in crawl spaces and such, there is no electric outlet for a plug. But there **is** a light socket. A socket-to-plug adaptor screws into a light socket and allows you to plug into it.

- **Screw driver** - To open access panels if necessary.

- **Phillips screw driver** - Same reason.

- **Small wrecking bar** - That's right. A wrecking bar. I'll remind you again that you're spending a lot of money. And I'll point out that sellers sometimes conceal defects by plastering over or boarding over them. When you find a suspicious area that you can't inspect, ask for permission to knock a hole. Offer to pay to have it repaired if necessary. But do not let some seller buffalo you into overlooking some serious defect by simply boarding it up.

- **Coveralls** - You may think the seller or Realtor® will laugh if you put on coveralls and crawl around in the crawl space. Again, I'll remind you that you're spending a lot of money. You look a horse in the mouth when you buy it. And you look an apartment building in the crawl space.

- **Boots or overshoes** - Same reason.

- **Hat** - Same reason.

- **Roll of paper towels** - To clean up after inspecting dirty areas.

- **Wet wipes** - Same reason.

Carry with you

- **Color camera** on a shoulder or neck strap. I prefer 35mm. You can get pictures developed in an hour these days. So you don't need to put up with the poor quality of instant cameras to see the pictures quickly. Photos can help in five ways:

  1. Remembering what you saw. Properties tend to blur together by the end of the day. An old Chinese saying points out that,

  The most faded ink [photograph] is better than the best memory.

  2. Mortgage application. If you plan to get institutional financing (as opposed to seller financing), you'll need photographs for the application.

  3. Partners. Use the pictures as part of your fund-raising effort if you are raising the money to buy the property through a partnership.

4. "Before pictures." If you plan to change the property physically, before and after photos are useful for establishing your track record to future prospective investors and lenders.

5. Lawsuits. I was recently sued and went to trial in a case where one of my tenants was assaulted by a rapist. Photos of the complex before the rape allegedly occurred were important, and in some cases could be crucial, to proving what conditions were at the time of a dispute.

• **Film** - Enough for 48 photos. Better to have too much than too little.

• **Flashbulbs** or electric flash.

• **Pen light**.

• **Measuring device**. This could be a measuring wheel on a stick. You roll it along the ceiling, floor, pavement, or whatever. An odometer-like meter gives you a rough measurement of the distance. Most real estate companies have one. Ask the agent or seller to carry it for you. Your hands will be full with your clipboard and pencil. They are made by Rolotape Corporation, 2701 North Van Marter Drive, Spokane, WA 99206 (509) 922-4114 and sold in surveyor's instrument stores. Nowadays, they also have electronic radar-like devices which can measure rooms.

• **Clipboard**.

• **Mechanical pencil**.

• **Note pad**.

• **This book**.

• **Light meter**. You need adequate exterior lighting. My insurance company recently had to pay a woman who sued me because of an assault which occurred in the bedroom of her apartment in my complex. Among other things, she alleged that the exterior lighting was inadequate. You want to know where you stand because an **over**lit building offers opportunities for conservation savings. And an **under**lit building has to be corrected. That's an expense which should result in a purchase price and cash down discount. You can buy a light meter at a photography shop. According to the Illuminating Engineering Society of North America and American National Standards Institute, the standard number of foot-candles you should have in multifamily parking lots is .6 (six-tenths).

• **Data gathering forms**. You will probably have a format for the way you analyze a prospective acquisition. This book can be used for that purpose to a large extent. But you may wish to consolidate some items on one sheet, or you may have special requirements not in here.

A smart seller or professional real estate agent will also have a check list to make sure they are prepared to show you the property. But not all sellers are smart. And not all real estate agents are professional. When they forget things, it wastes your time. So here's a check list of things to ask the seller or agent to bring.

- **Keys**. To every door that's locked. Including front door, all offices, basement, utility room, roof, etc.

- **Directions** to the property. If you're being taken by a salesman who has never been there before, it's best **not** to meet the agent or seller at the building you're inspecting unless there is a phone number there which either you or he could use to tell the other that he'll be late.

11

Night Inspection

Why a night inspection?

A building or a neighborhood can be a different place after hours when everyone is home than it was during the day when most residents were at work. Furthermore, you are buying a lighting system, in part, and you cannot evaluate a lighting system adequately in the day time.

Neighborhood

In general, look for **nuisances** which do not exist during the day time. For example, my mother lives on a quiet street. But if you look closely during the day, you'll notice a sign saying "No thru traffic." Mind you those signs do **not** say the common, "Not a through street." That would be false. It **is** a through street. The problem is the neighbors wish it weren't. That's because commuters roar up and down it every morning and evening to avoid a nearby street which jams up at rush hours.

See if the apartment building or neighborhood is a hang-out for undesirables after dark.

Friday or **Saturday** night would be the best time to make your night inspection. That's because the character of a neighborhood can change from week**day** to week**end** as well as from daylight to dark.

Singles bar

I once managed a 203-unit apartment complex. It was in a perfectly nice suburban neighborhood. A nighttime inspection would not have shown you anything unexpected...unless you came on Friday or Saturday nights. That's when the bar at the health club across the street attracted thousands of young singles.

The health club did not have enough parking for the singles. So they parked in our apartment parking lot. Our tenants, who had to drive a hundred yards or more away from their normal parking space on those nights, were livid and threatening to move out. We spoke to the club management but they offered little other than letting us put up signs in the rest rooms advising patrons that their cars would be towed if they were parked in the apartment complex's parking lot.

We had to issue bumper **decals** and dashboard **visitor passes** to our tenants. We had to block one of the two entrances to the parking lot and hire a security **guard** with a guard **dog** for Friday and Saturday nights...a substantial expense. (Guards with **guns** often get into altercations with problem visitors who go get their own gun. But guards with dogs hardly ever inspire problem visitors to go get their own **dog**.)

We arranged for a local tow truck to standby early in the evening with its flashing lights on. We put up "tenants and authorized guests only" signs.

In spite of all this we still had incidents like the drunk who thought it would be funny to urinate through the screen of one woman's apartment window onto her living room carpet.

Lights

Draw a diagram of the building and note the following on the diagram:

• **Parking areas:**

Size of fixtures _____

Type of fixtures _____

> In general, exterior incandescent fixtures should be replaced by fluorescent, sodium, or other types. That's because the rated life of incandescent bulbs is too short. For example, the typical par flood light lasts 2,000 hours. Other types last tens of thousands of hours. Short lives mean burned-out bulbs and burned-out bulbs risk injury and lawsuit liability. Being able to say you installed a high-pressure sodium bulb with a 24,000-hour life 3,000 hours ago may persuade a judge or jury that the bulb in question was burning on the night of an assault. Trying to prove that a flood light with a 2,000-hour life (about 200 days) was burning on a particular night is much harder.

Impression of adequacy_____

Light meter reading _____

Turned on/off by timer or photocell? _____

All lights which are turned on by timers should be switched to photocells. Timers get out of sync with the sun because of power outtages and the daily change in the time of sunup and sundown. As a result, they can cause you to waste electricity when they are on too long and may endanger your tenants when they are not on long enough.

• **Walkways:**

Size of fixtures _____

Type of fixtures _____

Impression of adequacy _____

Light meter reading _____

Turned on/off by timer or photocell? _____

• **Entryways:**

Size of fixtures _____

Type of fixtures _____

Impression of adequacy _____

Light meter reading _____

Turned on/off by timer or photocell? _____

• **Swimming pool:**

Size of fixtures_____

Type of fixtures _____

Impression of adequacy _____

Light meter reading _____

Underwater? _____

Turned on/off by timer or photocell? _____

• **Light from adjacent properties or streets:**

Size of fixtures _____

Type of fixtures _____

Impression of adequacy _____

Light meter reading _____

Turned on/off by timer or photocell? _____

Owned by whom? _____

• **Obstructions?** _____

_____

> Often, a building has adequate lighting when it is built. But as trees and shrubs grow, they begin to cast shadows. Owners and managers often fail to notice and correct the shadows because they grow so gradually. As the new owner, you would need to immediately either trim the trees or shrubs or increase the lighting to eliminate the shadows.

• **Dark areas where criminals could lurk?** _____

_____

Additional night inspection notes:

12

Exterior Inspection

Time to load your cameras

Load your camera. You'll be using it on the exterior. But don't get so engrossed in your photography that you forget to inspect the property with your **eyes**, too. Photographs have their place. But they are a poor substitute for eyes. Your main job is to inspect the property with your eyes. Not to take pictures of it. The photographs are secondary.

• **Front** of building - Take a **photo,** then inspect.

Make notes about the following:

• **Landscaping**_____

_____

> **Describe the shrubs, trees, and ground cover; their condition and improvement possibilities.**

📷 • **Signs** - Take a **photo** of each. _____

_____

_____

> Describe the type of sign, whether it's lit up at night, state of repair, and any improvement potential. Note whether there are <u>extraordinary</u> advertising signs. Buildings with high vacancy rates often employ the following unusual signs:
>
> - "Now Leasing" banners.
> - Strings of multicolored pennants.
> - Marquee on wheels advertising "specials."
> - "Burma Shave" style series of signs on sticks reciting apartment features.
> - Helium balloons.

• **Office hours** _____

> Apartment building leasing office hours are typically 9 to 6 daily. Longer hours generally indicate the building has a high vacancy rate. Shorter hours or "By appointment" in a complex with more than 75 or so units probably means less than 5% vacancy.

📷 • **Siding** - Take a **photo**.

Type _____

Condition _____

• **Windows**

Type (Storm or double-pane?) _____

Condition _____

_____

_____

> Make note of any windows which do not have either storm windows or double-pane glass unless the property is in an area where climate

control is a minor expense. This is easy to overlook. I once bought a home in New Jersey and didn't notice until <u>after</u> I moved in that there was no thermal glass. And I bought a Texas apartment building which had a house on the property. I failed to notice that the house had no storm windows, either!

• **Stairs** and stair railings - Take a **photo**.

Type _____

Condition _____

_____

_____

Note type and condition of both ground-level stairs built on slopes and stairs above ground level. Stairs and stair railings are safety-related items. Notes and photos you make as to their condition at the time you bought the property could become crucial in litigation over a subsequent injury.

• **Balconies** and railings

Type _____

Condition _____

_____

_____

Balconies and their railings are another safety-related item. Furthermore, they tend to deteriorate more rapidly than the building over time and are quite expensive to replace. Call your engineer's attention to any balconies and ask him to give a detailed account of their condition, design, safety, and replacement or repair cost.

• **Screens** _____

_____

_____

> **Make note of any windows which do not have screens. This is another one which is easy to overlook. That Texas house had no screens either.**

• **Drapes** _____

_____

> **Note the uniformity and appearance of the drapes.**

• **Roof**

Type _____

Age _____

Condition _____

_____

_____

> **If the roof is visible from the ground, note its type and approximate age. You may want to get your binoculars out of the car. Even an amateur can estimate the age of an asphalt or fiberglass shingle roof. They last about 20 years. If the building is 20 years old, it's probably got a very old roof or a very new one. Old shingle roofs look old.**
>
> **If the roof is flat, get a report from a roofing engineer without fail. Flat roofs leak even when new if they are not done just right. You can live with them, but only if they meet professional engineer specifications. If the roof was not installed correctly according to your engineer, figure on replacing it regardless of its age. That means deduct the cost of a new roof from the price and the down payment. If the seller balks at that but takes back a mortgage, put a clause in the mortgage which gives you the right to reduce the payments accordingly when the roof leaks. If he won't go for that, let someone else buy this problem property.**

• **Rain gutters** and downspouts _____

_____

_____

This is another easy-to-overlook item. <u>Broken</u> gutters, you'll notice. Gutters which <u>need paint</u>, you'll notice. But <u>missing</u> gutters...they're <u>invisible</u> unless you think about them.

- **Entrance door** - Take **photo**.

Type _____

Dimensions _____

Condition _____

Potential for improvement _____

Type of lock _____

Handicapped ramp? _____

Local law may require you to install a ramp for handicapped people, if there isn't one already there.

- **Garage** doors, if any - Take **photo**.

Number _____

Dimensions _____

Type _____

Potential for improvement _____

Type of lock _____

Condition _____

_____

_____

- **Sides and back** of the building - Take **photos**. _____

_____

_____

Recycle yourself through the check list items listed for the front of the building and check them again on the sides and back.

• Vending machines - Take photo. _____
_____

> **Note type, whether lit up, and whether extraordinary security measures, like a steel bar across the front, have been taken.**

• **Utility meters.**

Number _____
Type (gas, electric, or water)_____
Additional notes _____

> **Note which apartments or parts of the building the meters serve. This is important because later, you'll be asking the owner to show you his utility bills. If you fail to note the total number of meters, he may accidentally or intentionally deceive you by leaving some meters out.**

• **Air-conditioning** units.

Number _____
Brand _____
Model number(s) _____
Serial number(s) _____
Rated size _____
Location _____
Condition _____
_____
_____

> **The first four digits of the serial number tell you the week and year the unit was manufactured, e.g., 3383 means the 33rd week of 1983. Note whether they are located as to complicate groundskeeping.**

• **Swimming pool** - Take **photos**.

Width of pool_____

Length of pool _____

Shape of pool _____

Depths of pool _____

Dimensions of deck area _____

Is there a diving board? _____

> **Because of liability fears, landlords typically remove diving boards these days.**

Is there a fence around the pool?_____

Does the fence have a self-closing gate?_____

What is the condition of the pool surface underwater?_____

What type deck surface? _____

What is the condition of the deck surface? _____

Is there a life guard or an apparent place for one if the pool is closed at the time
   of your inspection? _____

Is there a pool water cover? Automated? _____

Data plate information from pool pump and filter _____

Fee income from tenants for using the pool? _____

Does the current owner allow non-tenants to use the pool? _____

Does the pool have an automatic chlorinator? _____

Is/how is the pool heated? _____

Is there a bubble cover or enclosure? _____

• **Pool furniture**

Number of chairs, type, and condition _____

_____

Number of tables, type, and condition _____

_____

Number of ash trays, type, and condition _____

_____

• **The look-down, walk-around.** _____

_____

_____

_____

> **Walk all over the grounds of the building...looking down. You're looking for <u>oddities</u>...like patches in the pavement or side walks, french drains, evidence of a trench that's been dug and refilled going through the lawn, etc. Whenever you find something, note it. And try to figure out why it's there. What's it near? Could there have been underground pipes leaking? Or a drainage problem in rainy weather? Problems which required excavation are often still not corrected or only partly corrected. And they tend to be very expensive. You want to know about them.**

• **Pavement** _____

_____

_____

> Asphalt is tricky. Concrete less so. If you have asphalt, you should get a paving engineer's report no matter how good it looks. As with flat roofs, even a brand new asphalt paving job can fail shortly after installation...if it wasn't done right. A paving engineer will take a core sample to see what's under the surface. If the pavement is concrete, you can generally tell yourself whether it's in good shape or not.

• **Parking**

Number of spaces _____

Dimensions of spaces _____

General quality of the tenants' vehicles _____

Dimensions of driving lanes _____

Covered or uncovered spaces? _____

Ownership of parking area _____

Make sure you'll <u>own</u> the parking which appears to come with the building. A *Wall Street Journal* article told about a small shopping center where not owning the parking area caused a big problem. The center's customers parked in the adjacent parking lot of a major retail chain store. That chain store put up a fence which made the center's customers have to walk hundreds of feet to get to the center if they parked in the chain store's lot. The center's business dropped off severely. If you will not own the parking spaces, make sure you get an easement which ensures your right to have your tenants park in the spaces in question.

• **Parking garage**

Height of lowest ceiling point _____

Lighting type _____

Lighting adequacy _____

Car heater outlets _____

In extremely cold climates, parking garage owners often provide electric outlets into which drivers plug their engine block heater.

Elevator - Use Chapter 19 on elevators in this book.

I suspect there is no "correct" ratio of parking spaces to units. It depends on the situation. The best way to find out if the parking is adequate is to ask the tenants. That's why that question is in the interview section of the book.

Have multi-story garages checked by an engineer. Steel reinforcing rods may have rusted out. If so, the structure is catastrophically dangerous and the problem is extremely expensive to repair.

• Snow and ice removal_____

_____

_____

Ask yourself what you're going to do with snow and ice (if you're in a climate where such occurs) come winter. Sloped, paved areas are an extreme hazard in icy weather. You must eliminate the hazard every time it freezes. That can be expensive and difficult on days when conditions prevent your nonresident staff (if any) from getting to the property. And you must have a place for the plow to pile the snow. That's easy to overlook if you inspect on a day when there is no snow.

• **Building dimensions** _____

_____

_____

Because so many apartment-building expense studies are done by the square foot, it's important that you get the area of the building right. A <u>survey</u> is the <u>best</u> way. But if you don't plan to get one, measure it yourself. Do <u>not</u> rely on anything given to you by the seller or his agent. Rolotape Corporation, which I mentioned makes measuring wheels, has a large, exterior version which has a bicycle wheel. At about $100, it's cheaper than a survey...and less accurate. You get what you pay for.

• **Lot dimensions** _____

_____

_____

Surveyors use the same bicycle measuring wheel often. But they take great pains to start in the right spot. Relying on where you <u>think</u> the boundaries are can throw you way off in some cases.

• **Trash** containers_____

_____

_____

Note whether it's in an enclosure, and if so, the type and condition of that enclosure. Note also the path of the truck that empties it. If it's too tight, fender-bender accidents to your tenants' cars will be common... until they move out. Or your building walls may be damaged by the truck. Note also whether the truck wheels are gouging the pavement. If so, you need to build a reinforced concrete pad where the wheels rest when lifting the container.

• **Fencing**

    Type _____

    Condition _____

    _____

    _____

• **Playground** _____

    _____

    _____

One could write an entire book on playgrounds. Indeed, they have. The two-volume *Handbook for Public Playground Safety*. It's available from the Consumer Product Safety Commission, Washington, DC 20207. Failure to comply with that *Handbook* will be used against you in court if there is an injury.

My standard suggestion on playgrounds in apartment complexes is to tear them down and replace them with a statue of a trial lawyer. Because if you don't, you will almost certainly be sued eventually by the parents of a child who gets injured in your playground. If you must buy an apartment building with a playground, get the above-mentioned *Handbook* and use it to see how much of the playground you'll be forced to change after closing.

• **Storage buildings** - Take **photos.** _____ 📷

    _____

    _____

I have found storage sheds and similar buildings to be of such limited value that I doubt they are worth having. I have had at least two sets of lawn-maintenance equipment (mower, weed-eater, edger, etc.) stolen from them. Fundamentally, the only thing you can store in them is stuff which cannot be pawned…like fertilizer, chlorine, or rock salt. Tools, light bulbs, mowers, etc., will all be stolen. The last time my lawn stuff was stolen (from a locked garage at my Texas apartment building), I decided to get out of the lawn care business. Instead, I hired a landscape service for $238 a month in summer and $100 a month in winter. That's for a 128' x 226' = 28,928 square foot property. At my California home, which is about 130' x 82' = 10,660 square feet, the gardener charges $140 a month year round.

Farming out lawn care also avoids the need for <u>dangerous materials</u> like gasoline and oil which can cause burn injuries or <u>contaminate</u> the soil. And elimination of lawn care duties lowers your payroll and therefore your <u>workers compensation</u> costs (assuming your lawn-care subcontractor provides proof of such insurance).

• **Mailboxes** - Take **photos**.

Number _____

Type_____

Condition _____

_____

_____

• **Power lines and substations**—Draw **map** showing relationship to subject property

In the **12/31/90** *Fortune* magazine, David Lewis, a Houston real estate consultant said houses near power lines had dropped **25%** in value in the previous 18 months. A Manhattan real estate risk advisory service now tells investors where electrical substations are so investors can avoid those neighborhoods. As far as I can tell, power lines and substations pose no threat to health. But hysteria which thinks they do can adversely affect your financial health. If you buy properties near power lines and substations, you'd better get an appropriate discount until people stop fearing them.

Additional exterior inspection notes:

13

General

Room inspection check lists

One problem with room inspections is that it is easy to overlook things that seem obvious **after** settlement. For example, many investors learn too late that a building has no storm windows or that there is no heat in the kitchen. Sometimes, the investor's eye is distracted by an object or feature in the room, and he never looks at the ceiling or in the closet, thereby overlooking a bad water stain.

Sellers, tenants, and real estate agents often make the prospective buyer feel he is intruding and subtly (or not so subtly) try to rush him through the property.

Each of these problems can be eliminated or minimized by a thorough check list which is religiously used during inspections. The following room check lists are, in part, lists of obvious features, such as ceilings and walls. These items are included to insure that the inspector carefully **looks** at all parts (even the obvious ones!) of each room he visits. The check lists are grouped by room because the actual inspection will be made room by room.

Overview

• Is the room arrangement sensible? _____

Is the kitchen next to a bathroom? _____

Must a person pass through one bedroom to get into another? _____

_____

> **These two awkward juxtapositions violate FHA standards.**

• Is there more than one exit for third-floor and higher apartments? (Check local fire code if not.) _____

• Is there storage for bicycles, snow tires? _____

• Is there closet space near the entrance for coats? _____

• Is there a linen closet? _____

General notes on the building:

14

Living room

• **Dimensions** _____

• **Walls**

Type_____

Are they vertical as indicated by a level? _____

Any chance they contain asbestos? _____

Enough unbroken wall for a sofa?_____

Condition _____

_____

_____

• Ceiling

Type (acoustic tile? plaster?)_____

Height (8'? 10'? etc.) _____

Any chance it contains asbestos? _____

Condition (falling down? sound? stained?)_____

_____

_____

• Floor

Type_____

Check if the floor is level _____

Any chance it contains asbestos? _____

Condition _____

_____

_____

• Light switches

Type_____

Condition _____

_____

_____

• Light fixtures

Type_____

Condition _____

_____

_____

• Woodwork

Finish _____

Any chance of lead-based paint? _____

Condition _____

_____

_____

• Doors

Stops on all doors to protect walls? _____

Check if vertical with level _____

• Door locks

Type _____

Condition _____

_____

_____

• Security peephole or window at entrance? _____

• Heat

Type _____

Is it adequate? _____

_____

• Thermostat

Type _____

Test response time _____

_____

• Windows

Function smoothly? _____

Type_____

Condition _____

_____

_____

Storm windows (all panes intact?) _____

_____

_____

Screens _____

_____

_____

• **Window locks**

Type_____

Condition _____

_____

_____

• **Window/glass door covering** (drapes, blinds, etc.)

Type_____

Condition _____

_____

_____

• **Electric outlets**

Number _____

Adequacy_____

_____

There should be one every 12 feet or so.

• **Fireplace**

Type _____

Screen and utensils included? _____

Condition _____

_____

_____

• **Telephone jack?** _____

• **Cable TV jack?** _____

Additional notes on living room:

15

Kitchen

• **Dimensions** _____

• **Walls**

    Type_____

    Are they vertical as indicated by a level? _____

    Any chance they contain asbestos? _____

    Enough unbroken wall for a sofa?_____

    Condition _____

    _____

    _____

• Ceiling

Type (acoustic tile? plaster?) _____

Height (8'? 10'? etc.) _____

Any chance it contains asbestos? _____

Condition (falling down? sound? stained?) _____

_____

_____

• Floor

Type _____

Check if the floor is level _____

Any chance it contains asbestos? _____

Condition _____

_____

_____

• Light switches

Type _____

Condition _____

_____

_____

• Light fixtures

Type _____

Condition _____

_____

_____

• Woodwork

Finish _____

Any chance of lead-based paint? _____

Condition _____

_____

_____

• Electric outlets

Number _____

Adequacy _____

> **There should be one every six feet or so.**

• Cabinets - Take photos.

Type _____

Color _____

Drawers and doors operate properly? _____

Condition _____

_____

_____

• Counter top

Type _____

Color _____

Condition _____

_____

_____

• Sink

Type _____

Color _____

Condition _____

_____

_____

> There are three types of sinks: stainless steel, which is recommended for apartments, porcelain-coated steel, and porcelain-coated cast iron. Porcelain-coated steel should be avoided because it chips easily and can't be completely repaired. Cast iron also chips but much less frequently. You can tell the difference by tapping them. Steel sounds thin and tinny. If you aren't confident of your ability to tell the difference, visit a plumbing supply house and ask a salesperson to show you both kinds. A porcelain-coated steel sink is a corner-cutting choice. When you find one, there are probably many other cheaper construction features, both visible and hidden in the building.

• Range and oven

Type _____

Color _____

Number _____

Size _____

Age _____

Condition, inside and out _____

_____

_____

• Range hood

Light _____

Self-vented or exterior vent _____

Check operation of fan _____

• Exhaust fan (functions smoothly?) _____

• Microwave oven (Built-in)

Brand _____

Model _____

Serial number _____

Condition _____

_____

_____

• Refrigerator

Owned by tenant? _____

Brand _____

Model (size) _____

Serial number _____

Color _____

Number _____

Age _____

Water line available for ice maker? _____

Condition _____

_____

_____

• Dishwasher

Owned by tenant? _____

Brand _____

Model (size) _____

Serial number _____

Color _____

Number _____

Age _____

Condition _____

_____

_____

• Trash compactor

Owned by tenant? _____

Brand _____

Model (size)_____

Serial number _____

Color _____

Number _____

Age _____

Condition _____

_____

_____

> **You want brand, model and serial numbers on anything that can be taken out between your initial inspection and closing. Sellers have been known to strip properties or to replace the appliances you inspected with lower quality versions.**

• Other appliances

Type_____

Color _____

Condition _____

_____

_____

• Are any appliances or light fixtures not included in the sale of the house?

_____

_____

_____

> **This must be specified in the listing agreement and carried over to the purchase agreement. It is common for house deals to blow up temporarily when the buyer learns belatedly that certain drapes, blinds, shrubs, or light fixtures are not included in the deal.**

• **Doorstops on all doors?** _____

• **Adequate storage space?** _____

HUD Minimum Property Standards for Kitchens			
Kitchen Size	Shelving	Drawer Space	Counter Top
40-60 sq.ft.	30 sq.ft.	5 sq.ft.	6 sq.ft.
Over 60 sq.ft.	54 sq.ft.	10 sq.ft.	12 sq.ft.

• **Faucet**

Type _____

Water cutoff valves? _____

Test for rusty water, temperature, pressure _____

Condition _____

_____

_____

> **Cutoffs are valves (on the supply lines under the sink) that are used to shut off the water when the plumbing is being repaired. Lack of cutoff valves is generally a sign of cheap construction.**

• **Disposer**

Brand _____

Model _____

Test operation _____

> **Some disposers are more easily repaired than others, and the difference can mean more than $100 per unit when repairs are needed. Check with knowledgeable local apartment operators to learn which are best.**

• **Windows**

Function smoothly? _____

Type _____

Condition _____

_____

_____

Storm windows (all panes intact?) _____

_____

_____

Screens _____

_____

_____

• **Window locks**

Type _____

Condition _____

_____

_____

• **Window coverings** (drapes, blinds, etc.)

Type _____

Condition _____

_____

_____

• **Exterior door**

Type _____

Storm door? _____

Condition _____

_____

_____

• **Door locks**

Type_____

Condition _____

_____

_____

• **Heat source**

Type_____

Adequate? _____

• **Telephone jack?** _____

• **Cable TV jack?** _____

Additional notes on kitchen:

16

Bathrooms

• Floor

Type_____

Check if the floor is level _____

Any chance it contains asbestos? _____

Condition _____

_____

_____

• Ceiling

Type_____

Any chance it contains asbestos? _____

Condition _____

_____

_____

• Walls

Type_____

Check with level to see if vertical _____

Condition _____

_____

_____

• Toilet

Is the toilet a water-saver model? _____

Color _____

Age _____

Seat condition _____

Condition _____

_____

_____

You can generally find the age of the toilet stamped on the underside of the top of the tank. This is often also the year the building was constructed.

• Lavatory sink

Color _____

Size _____

Age _____

Vanity _____

Condition _____

_____

_____

Faucet type _____

Faucet condition _____

Test water for rust and pressure _____

> **Turn on the hot water and hold your hand under it to see how long it takes to get hot. (It shouldn't take more than eight to ten seconds.) Also check for rust in the water. Test the water pressure by turning on the tub and the sink's cold water, then flush the toilet. If the pressure is inadequate, the faucet flow will be reduced by the flush.**

Cutoff valves? _____

Plug _____

Drain speed _____

• Medicine cabinet

Size _____

Condition _____

_____

_____

• Tub

Type _____

Color _____

Size _____

Age _____

Condition _____

_____

_____

> **There are three major types of tubs: fiberglass, porcelain-coated cast iron, and porcelain-coated steel. As in kitchen sinks, porcelain-coated steel is a cheaper model which is prone to chipping. Fiber glass makes an excellent tub, but it can be scratched easily by cleansers. Unfortunately, tenants seem to inevitably forget warnings against using cleansers, and the damage is irreparable.**

• Tub wall

Type_____

Condition _____

_____

_____

• Shower

Glass door? _____

Curtain? _____

Shower nozzle type _____

Shower valve type _____

Test hot water for rust and delay time _____

Test cold water for rust _____

Drain plug _____

Drain speed _____

Condition _____ _____

_____

_____

• Access panel for shower valves

Type of pipe _____

Evidence of leaks?_____

Condition _____

_____

_____

• Window

Function smoothly? _____

Type_____

Storm window intact? _____

Screen? _____

Condition _____

_____

_____

• Window lock

Type _____

Condition _____

_____

_____

• Woodwork condition _____

• Exhaust fan functioning smoothly? _____

• Heat adequate? _____

• Towel bar condition _____

• Toilet paper holder condition _____

• Door

Type _____

Doorstop on door? _____

Condition _____

_____

_____

• Door Lock

Type _____

Condition _____

_____

_____

• **Light fixture** adequate? _____

• **Electric outlets**

    Number _____

    Adequate? _____

> **Modern building codes generally call for outlets with built-in circuit breakers in bathrooms because of the possibility that water might complete a circuit thereby electrocuting someone.**

• **Telephone jack?** _____

Additional notes on bathroom:

17

Bedrooms

• **Dimensions** _____

Big enough for queen or king size bed? _____

• **Walls**

Type _____
Are they vertical as indicated by a level? _____
Any chance they contain asbestos? _____
Condition _____
_____
_____

• Ceiling

Type (acoustic tile? plaster?)_____

Height (8'? 10'? etc.) _____

Any chance it contains asbestos? _____

Condition (falling down? sound? stained?)_____

_____

_____

• Floor

Type_____

Check if the floor is level _____

Any chance it contains asbestos? _____

Condition _____

_____

_____

• Closet space adequate? _____

> **A modern bedroom should have at least five feet of closets which are a least two feet deep.**

• Light switches

Type_____

Condition _____

_____

_____

• Light fixtures

Type_____

Condition _____

_____

_____

• Woodwork

Finish _____

Any chance of lead-based paint? _____

Condition _____

_____

_____

• Doors

Type _____

Stops on all doors to protect walls? _____

Check if vertical with level _____

Condition _____

_____

_____

• Door lock

Type _____

Condition _____

_____

_____

• Heat adequate? _____

• Thermostat

Type _____

Test response time _____

_____

• Windows

Function smoothly? _____

Type_____

Condition _____

_____

_____

Storm windows (all panes intact?) _____

_____

_____

Screens _____

_____

_____

• Window locks

Type_____

Condition _____

_____

_____

• Window/glass door covering (drapes, blinds, etc.)

Type_____

Included in purchase price? _____

Condition _____

_____

_____

• Electric outlets

Number _____

Adequacy_____

• Telephone jack? _____

• Cable TV jack? _____

Additional notes on bedroom:

18

Basement, Utility Room, Crawl Space

This phase of your overall inspection should be **last** to avoid tracking dirt through the house or apartments and halls. This is a sort of **amateur** check list for **screening** purposes only. You should have an **expert** inspect the property and he should have his own, more detailed check lists.

• Wall

Type_____

Check if vertical with level _____

Evidence of termite treatment? _____

_____

Condition _____

_____

_____

Treatment for termites generally involves drilling holes in the basement wall at intervals of about one foot all the way around the building. After insecticide is sprayed through, the worker plugs the holes. When you see evidence of treatment, look especially hard for termite damage that has not been adequately repaired or is irreparable.

• **Sill plate** damaged by termites or dry rot? _____

• **Joists**

    Size _____

    Spacing _____

    Condition _____

    _____

    _____

Check for cracks, dry rot, and termites.

• **Wiring**

    Type (Knob-and-tube, copper, wiring) _____

    Condition _____

    _____

    _____

There are several types of wiring, and older buildings are likely to have a combination of them all. "Knob-and-tube" wiring is characterized by cloth-insulated wiring that is twisted around porcelain knobs. Whenever the wire must pass through wood, it is encased in a porcelain tube. Knob-and-tube wiring is often a fire hazard and will have to be replaced if modern appliances, such as air conditioners or electric ranges, are to be used. Modern wiring features plastic insulation which is sometimes further protected by metal sheathing.

Aluminum wiring can also be a fire hazard. There was a copper shortage from 1965 to 1973. As a result, a lot of buildings which were built or rewired then have ALUMINUM WIRING. How can you tell?

You can look at the exposed wires in a switch or outlet . Aluminum is silver or white; copper, brown. Also, the letters "AL" are usually printed on aluminum wire's plastic covering.

The U.S. Consumer Product Safety Commission (CPSC) says that buildings with pre-1973 aluminum wiring are 55 times more likely to reach fire hazard stage than buildings wired with copper wire. Of course, buildings wired with copper wire are not likely to reach fire hazard stage at all so 55 times nearly zero is not much higher than zero. Post 1973 aluminum wire is safer because of improvements in its design.

In addition to the safety concerns, aluminum wiring may adversely affect your ability to sell, refinance, or insure your building. That is, many buyers, lenders, and insurers redline buildings with aluminum wiring. Some insurers charge increased premiums...as much as quadruple the copper-wiring rate.

That's an overreaction. The CPSC says the increased fire hazard can be eliminated by "crimp connection." That is, you have to redo all the connections: in every switch, outlet, fixture, and splice. "Crimp connection" is done with a special tool called a Copalum parallel splice connector and special metal sleeves. A.M.P. Special Industries of Valley Forge, PA is the only manufacturer of the tool.

• **Separate meters** for each apartment and one for the owner? _____

If tenants share meters with each other or if a tenant pays for common items, such as hall lighting or the oil burner motor, there will be bad feelings that will probably necessitate the installation of additional meters. Deceitful wiring is another problem you may encounter. This places one tenant's circuit on another's meter or, more frequently, places some of the owner's circuits on his tenants' meters. The tenant eventually finds out when he blows a fuse and notices that the hall lights also went out. Replacement of the fuse brings light to the halls and an angry contact to the owner.

• **Plumbing**

Type_____

Evidence of leaks _____

Evidence of flooding _____

_____

Evidence of flooding includes water lines on walls, supports, equipment; fresh paint which may be covering up a water line; rust on lower portions of metal fixtures; sump pump; and difficulty in arranging inspections during or after wet weather.

• Heating system

Type _____

Age _____

Condition _____

_____

_____

The date of manufacturer is often on the data plate. Sometimes it's in code. For example, on air-conditioners, the first four digits of the serial number are the week and year it was manufactured, e.g., "3385" would mean built in the 33rd week of 1985.

Copy down all data plate information _____

_____

_____

Fuel _____

Condition of combustion chamber _____

Type of piping _____

Blower motor? _____

Pipe insulation? _____

If the pipe insulation is white and gypsum-like in appearance, it may contain asbestos. Have it checked.

Low-water cutoff valve? _____

A low-water cutoff is a safety device that turns off the heater if the amount of water drops below a safe level. Low water cutoff valves are often required by local law and/or by insurance companies.

Heater insulated? _____

Look for asbestos.

Evidence of repairs or leaks? _____

Capacity of oil storage tanks, if any _____

Standard residential tanks hold 275 gallons; buried tanks 550 or more. The greater the capacity, the better, since your oil dealer can make fewer stops. But buried tanks are now a very scary environmental hazard. You need to make sure any buried tanks have never leaked. State and federal laws now require registration, monitoring, etc. of underground storage tanks. They may no longer be worth the hassle in most cases.

Oil dealer name _____

Dealers usually put an advertising sticker on the tank or heater. Copy down the name and phone number for expense verification later.

• Air-conditioner compressor

Copy down every thing on the data plate _____

_____

_____

I once bought a building with a 40-ton air-conditioner. We did not have a manual, so I wrote to the manufacturer to see if I could get one. They not only sent me one, they told me the date mine had been installed, the installer, etc.

Water treatment? _____

> **Water treatment equipment is necessary in areas where the water quality is less than ideal. Without water treatment, the condenser pipes clog up like hardening of the arteries. Which is expensive to fix. Lack of water treatment may indicate the compressor and condenser you are acquiring will need major overhauls.**

Condition _____

_____

_____

• Support columns

Type _____
Condition _____

_____

_____

• Outside door

Type _____
Check if door is vertical with level _____
Condition _____

_____

_____

• Door Lock

Type _____
Condition _____

_____

_____

• Steps

Is there a hand rail? _____

Condition _____

_____

_____

> **Hand rails are often required by law and/or lenders.**

• Ceiling

Height _____

Fire-resistant material? _____

> **Fire-resistant basement ceilings are required by law in many localities. Specially treated sheetrock can be used for this purpose.**

• Electric service panel

Fuses or circuit breakers? _____

Capacity_____

> **Capacity is measured in amperes. The rated capacity should be written somewhere on the service panel. Do not rely on the fuses' rated amperage because someone may have installed fuses of the wrong size.**

• Gas meters

Number (one for each apartment?) _____ __

• Water service

Type of pipe _____

Size _____

> Copper pipes are best. Galvanized pipes deteriorate with age and may have to be replaced.

• **Hot-water heaters**

Type of fuel _____

Number of units_____

Capacity in gallons _____

> You should have a capacity of about ten gallons per person and ten gallons per washing machine (more for machines in common laundry rooms). For example, a two-bedroom apartment which will house two or three people needs about 30 gallons of hot water capacity.

Age _____

> Hot water heaters last about 10 to 15 years. Look for the installation or manufacture date to determine the remaining life.

Aquastat setting_____

> The aquastat setting determines the temperature of the hot water. It should be no more than 140 degrees Fahrenheit. A hotter setting could be an indication that your heater has inadequate capacity or that you could lower the utility bill by lowering the setting. Tenants who receive very hot water adjust their hot water faucets down to avoid being burned; less hot water is used, and the capacity of the heater is stretched. If there are <u>dishwashers</u> in the building, the water must be at least 140 degrees Fahrenheit for dishes to be properly cleaned.

Pressure relief valve _____

- **Air ducts**

  Fabric noise insulation?_____

  Any chance insulation contains asbestos?_____

> If the building has warm-air heat or air conditioning, there will be air ducts. Quality installations have a fabric sleeve near the beginning of the duct work to prevent blower machine noise from rattling the entire duct system. Ducts should go to outside walls if they are to heat or cool most efficiently. Ducts which go only to the inner walls are initially cheaper but more costly in the long run.

- **Drains**

  Floor sloped to be sure no ponds will form? _____

- **Windows**

  Type_____

  Do they leak?_____

- **Window Locks**

  Type_____

  Condition _____

- **Crawl space** and vapor barrier _____

> A vapor barrier is plastic or tar paper unrolled to cover the ground in a crawl space. You can uncover a lot of information in a basement or crawl space. Always inspect dark areas. Use the light in your inspection kit and wear coveralls and a painter's hat to make a thorough inspection of such places. Observe every feature, keeping in mind that there is a <u>reason </u>for each. Is there an extra column which appears to have been added after construction? Why? Are the walls or partitions sheetrocked over? Why? Sheetrock and paneling have often been used to cover severe damage. Tactfully question the owner about the things you can't figure out.

• **Insulation** under first floor? _____

> If the space under the first floor is unheated, the floor should be insulated. Buildings built before the '70s energy crisis often did not have insulation under the first floor.

• **Earthquake** strengthening

Sill plate bolted to foundation every four feet and within one foot of each corner?

_____

Plywood sheathing or diagonal bracing on studs from sill plate to first floor?

_____

Masonry chimneys tied into structure with steel straps? _____

• **Lawn sprinkler system**

Number of stations? _____

Number of times on per day? _____

Duration for each station? _____

• **Transformer?** _____

> Transformers often contain PCBs. If there is a transformer in the building you are considering buying, find out from the electric company if it contains PCBs. If it does, talk to an environmental expert about the risks.

Additional notes on basement, utility room, and crawl space:

19

Common Area

Common areas are hallways, lobbies, stairways, and so forth.

• Walls

Type_____

Check with level to see if vertical _____

Any chance they contain asbestos? _____

Condition _____

_____

_____

• Ceiling

Type_____

Any chance it contains asbestos? _____

Condition _____

_____

_____

• Floors

Type_____

Check with level to see if sloped _____

Any chance it contains asbestos? _____

Condition _____

_____

_____

• Stairways (condition) _____

_____

_____

• Fire extinguishers

Number _____

Location_____

_____

Inspection current? _____

_____

• Mailboxes - Take photos.

Type_____

Proper number? _____

Condition _____

_____

_____

[camera] • **Announcement box** - Take **photos.**

Condition _____

> Most states and many municipalities require landlords to post various notices in the common areas of the building. An announcement box should be available for this purpose.

• **Light fixtures**

Type _____
Condition _____

• **Smoke detectors**

Number (adequate?) _____
Test to see if working properly _____

• **Doorbells**

Appearance _____
Operation _____

• **Intercom**

Speakers function properly? _____
Remote door-openers function properly? _____
Appearance _____
_____

[camera] • **Common laundry room** - Take **photos.**

Dimensions _____

Washers

Number _____

Data plate information _____

Charge per wash _____

Condition _____

_____

_____

Dryers

Number _____

Data plate information _____

Charge per time unit of drying _____

Type of fuel used _____

Vented where? _____

Condition _____

_____

_____

Lighting

Type _____

How switched on and off? (timer?) _____

Visibility? _____

Visibility should allow people outside the laundry room to be able to observe any person committing a crime in the laundry room.

Drain in floor? _____

Table for folding? _____

Ceiling

Type_____

Any chance it contains asbestos? _____

Condition _____

_____

_____

Walls

Type_____

Condition _____

_____

_____

Floor

Type_____

Any chance of asbestos? _____

Condition _____

_____

_____

Heat adequate? _____

> **In cold climates, laundry rooms may need heat above and beyond that provided by the washers and dryers to prevent pipes from freezing and for user comfort.**

Additional notes on common areas:

20

Elevators

Take **photos** of the wall and cab control panel.

• **Number** of elevators_____

• **Door dimensions** _____

• **Cab interior dimensions** _____

> **Dimensions are important because furniture and equipment must fit into at least one of the building's elevators when tenants move in. When furniture or equipment is too big to fit inside the elevators, the movers override the normal elevator controls so they can put the item on top of the elevator...usually with a moving man riding there to hold it. They charge extra for that. Low ceiling is the main problem. You ought to have at least one elevator with a ceiling height of at least 14 feet.**

• **Manufacturer** _____

• **Cable or hydraulic elevator?** _____

> A cable elevator is pulled up by a cable attached to its top. A hydraulic elevator is pushed up by a plunger attached to its bottom. Most elevators are cable. Hydraulic is not recommended over 5 stories.

• **Cab ceiling**

    Type_____

    Condition _____

    _____

    _____

• **Cab walls**

    Type_____

    Condition _____

    _____

    _____

• **Cab floor**

    Type_____

    Condition _____

    _____

    _____

> Ratty-looking elevators can be dramatically renovated relatively cheaply by replacing the surface of the interior walls, floor, and ceiling and by replacing the face of the control panel and control buttons.

Additional elevator notes:

PART SIX: INTERVIEWS

21

Interviews

The most important part of this book

This chapter is the most important part of this book. I've never done it, but I would almost be willing to buy an existing building **sight-unseen**...if only I could **interview** the appropriate people beforehand.

This chapter will discuss the **important questions to ask, and to whom** to ask the questions. Each question will indicate the recommended interviewee. In the Appendixes at the back of this book, you will find the questions grouped by interviewee for your convenience in using the questions.

There are eight categories of people you want to interview:

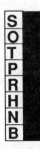

- Seller
- Previous owner
- Tenants
- Property manager
- Resident manager
- HVAC contractor, if any
- Neighbors
- Buyers who have bought from this seller

Of these, the **tenants** are the **most important**. In fact, interviewing the tenants is absolutely **crucial**. I would not buy any building where I was prevented from interviewing the tenants.

There are one or more code letters with each of the following questions. The code letters tell you to whom that question should be directed. In many cases, the same question should be put to more than one category.

What if the real estate agent or seller won't let you talk to the these people?

The agent has no such right. The **seller** has the right to prevent you from talking to his tenants, property manager or HVAC contractor. If the seller exercises that right, buy a different property.

Interview questions

• From whom did you buy the property?_____ `S O T P R H N B`

_____

> **If you can't get this information from the seller, it's in the county hall of records.**

• Why are you selling the property? _____ `S O T P R H N B`

_____

> **Some sellers will refuse to answer. That's OK. And other sellers will give you false answers. But you should always try to figure out the seller's motivation because it may help you in the negotiations...or convince you to look elsewhere.**

• What do you plan to do with the sale proceeds?_____ `S O T P R H N B`

_____

> **Same as the previous question.**

• Will this sale be part of an exchange? _____ `S O T P R H N B`

> If so, you know part of the seller's motivation. Exchangers are tax conscious. Consequently, many will also be receptive to an installment sale. (They should **not** be receptive to an installment sale. See my book *Aggressive Tax Avoidance for Real Estate Investors* for an explanation.)

S O T P R H N B • Have you had any roof leaks? _____

_____

_____

> Flat roofs are common on apartment buildings. They can drive you nuts. Even pitched roofs can drive you nuts if they're not flashed right. And many buildings have jazzy, partly vertical, pitched roofs which increase the probability of leaks. Get a roofing engineer to give you a report on any flat roof you are considering buying. You do **not** need a report on a pitched roof unless there are problems with it. Note that many buildings have combination flat and pitched roofs. Often, the roof is pitched until it gets to the middle. There, you find a parapet wall and a flat roof under the HVAC equipment. Partly-flat roofs cause problems the same as completely flat roofs. Of course, you should get details on any leaks the interviewee reports.

S O T P R H N B • Have you had any underground pipe leaks? _____

_____

S O T P R H N B • Have you had any underground tank leaks? _____

_____

> These are usually quite expensive to fix. Check them out thoroughly.

S O T P R H N B • Have you had pests?

Termites? _____

Roaches? _____

Mice? _____

Rats? _____

Any other vermin? _____

• Have you had any problems with the air-conditioning system? _____   `S` `O` `T` `P` `R` `H` `N` `B`

_____

• Have you had any crime in the neighborhood or in the building?   `S` `O` `T` `P` `R` `H` `N` `B`

_____

• Have you had any plumbing problems? _____   `S` `O` `T` `P` `R` `H` `N` `B`

• How many (which) apartments, if any, have furniture rented from the owner of the   `S` `O` `T` `P` `R` `H` `N` `B`
   building? _____

• Is there flooding in the basement or elsewhere on or near the property during or after   `S` `O` `T` `P` `R` `H` `N` `B`
   heavy rains? _____

> **This is an extremely important question. One apartment building I managed had a parking lot which flooded up to glove compartment depth about once a month. The dumpster would float away from its spot and we'd have to push it back before the water went down leaving it out in the middle of the parking lot. Drainage problems are extremely difficult and costly to correct. They are also extremely easy to overlook even in the most thorough physical inspection...but every tenant in the building knows about the problem. They'll be glad to tell you about it...if only you ask.**

• Are there any tenants you wish were not here? _____   `S` `O` `T` `P` `R` `H` `N` `B`

_____

_____

> **The seller and property manager may lie about problem tenants. The previous owner's information may be out of date. And the tenants may be reluctant to complain. Do your best to get honest answers to this question. Problem tenants can be costly. If you have a suspicion you may not be getting all the information you need, you might track down a tenant who recently moved out and ask him or her.**

• Do you have any parking problems? _____   `S` `O` `T` `P` `R` `H` `N` `B`

_____

> **Also very costly and very easy to overlook but known to all tenants.**

`S O T P R H N B` • Have you had any trash removal/dumpster problems? _____
_____

`S O T P R H N B` • Is the air-conditioning adequate? _____

`S O T P R H N B` • Are your appliances all in good working order? _____

`S O T P R H N B` • Have you had any drain stoppages? _____

`S O T P R H N B` • Do your intercom and remote door opener work properly? _____

`S O T P R H N B` • Have you had any snow removal/ice problems? _____

> **They laugh when I ask this in Texas. But it seems they have ice storms almost every year. Darned if I can figure out what's so funny.**

`S O T P R H N B` • Have you had any problems with elevator service? _____
_____

> **Be especially alert for inadequate capacity (overly long waits for an elevator). It's next to impossible to correct. The other main problem is frequent down-time.**

`S O T P R H N B` • Is the building exterminated regularly? _____

> **If so, make sure you figure on that expense.**

`S O T P R H N B` • Have you had any problems with smog in the area? _____
_____

• Is there a noise problem in the building or in the neighborhood? _____ S O T P R H N B

_____

• Have you had any problems with the janitorial service? _____ S O T P R H N B

_____

• What rent do you pay? _____ S O T P R H N B

> **You should ask even though the seller has already told you. Sellers lie sometimes.**

• Did you receive, or are you going to receive, any rent concessions? _____ S O T P R H N B

_____

> **Rent concessions are very common nowadays. I think the main reason landlords give rent concessions instead of lowering the rent is that they think buyers like you will be dumb enough not to ask the tenants if they got any concessions to get them to sign the lease. Don't be that dumb.**

• How much is your security deposit? _____ S O T P R H N B

• Do you plan to renew your lease when it expires? _____ S O T P R H N B

• Are you satisfied with the performance of the manager? _____ S O T P R H N B

_____

_____

• Is the exterior lighting adequate? _____ S O T P R H N B

• Are the laundry facilities adequate? _____ S O T P R H N B

• Have you made any improvements to your apartment? _____ S O T P R H N B

• Does your water ever have an odor or color? _____ S O T P R H N B

`[S][O][T][P][R][H][N][B]` • Do you rent the furniture in the apartment? _____

`[S][O][T][P][R][H][N][B]` • Do any of your toilets run continuously? _____

`[S][O][T][P][R][H][N][B]` • Do any of your faucets drip? _____

`[S][O][T][P][R][H][N][B]` • Do the apartments' trash containers generally have enough room for your trash?
_____

`[S][O][T][P][R][H][N][B]` • Are you satisfied with the policies which govern the swimming pool? _____
_____

`[S][O][T][P][R][H][N][B]` • Do you know of any safety hazards on the property? _____
_____

`[S][O][T][P][R][H][N][B]` • Are your door locks adequate? _____

`[S][O][T][P][R][H][N][B]` • Are your window locks adequate? _____

> **The tenant's answer to these last three questions could become important in subsequent litigation. You also need to know the answer so you can estimate how much it will cost to put the property in adequate shape.**

`[S][O][T][P][R][H][N][B]` • Do you have a waiting list? _____

> **If the answer is yes, rents are probably below market.**

`[S][O][T][P][R][H][N][B]` • Which oil dealer do you use? (where applicable) _____
_____

`[S][O][T][P][R][H][N][B]` • How many electric, gas, and water meters do you have? _____

> **Compare this number with the bills to make sure you account for all expenses.**

• Have you appealed your property tax assessment? If so, what were the results?   `S` `O` `T` `P` `R` `H` `N` `B`

_____

_____

• Do you allow pets? _____   `S` `O` `T` `P` `R` `H` `N` `B`

• Have you had any problems with the heating system? _____   `S` `O` `T` `P` `R` `H` `N` `B`

_____

> **One of the most common problems...and one which is difficult to fix...is some apartments being too hot and others being too cold...usually due to the uneven effects of the sun.**

• Have you had any problems with the electrical system? _____   `S` `O` `T` `P` `R` `H` `N` `B`

_____

> **From the tenant's standpoint, these usually manifest themselves as blown circuit breakers.**

• Is there enough hot water? _____   `S` `O` `T` `P` `R` `H` `N` `B`

• Is there adequate water pressure? _____   `S` `O` `T` `P` `R` `H` `N` `B`

> **If there isnt, you may only need a new line in from the street. Or you may need an entire new plumbing system.**

• Why did you sell? _____   `S` `O` `T` `P` `R` `H` `N` `B`

• When did you sell? _____   `S` `O` `T` `P` `R` `H` `N` `B`

• What were the price and terms? _____   `S` `O` `T` `P` `R` `H` `N` `B`

> **Be especially alert for balloon payments falling due in the near future. These put pressure on the seller.**

|S|O|T|P|R|H|N|B| • What was your asking price? _____

|S|O|T|P|R|H|N|B| • Do you remember the buyer's first offer? _____

> **This gives you an idea of the seller's negotiating style.**

|S|O|T|P|R|H|N|B| • Were there any problems in the negotiations? _____

|S|O|T|P|R|H|N|B| • Were there problems with the property which you feel the seller should have told you about beforehand? _____

_____

|S|O|T|P|R|H|N|B| • Have you had any problems with the previous owner since you bought it?

_____

|S|O|T|P|R|H|N|B| • Would you do business with him again? _____

> **You're trying to find out if the guy you're dealing with pulls any stunts like getting you to commit then threatening to pull out unless you grant him some eleventh-hour concession. Don't deal with those kinds of people.**

|S|O|T|P|R|H|N|B| • Were there any problems on closing day? _____

_____

|S|O|T|P|R|H|N|B| • Would you be willing to own the property again? _____
If not, why not? _____

_____

_____

• How well has the heating system been maintained? _____ S O T P R H N B

_____

• How well has the air-conditioning system been maintained? _____ S O T P R H N B

_____

• When were the following last replaced?   S O T P R H N B

    Roof _____

    Boiler _____

    Air-conditioner compressor _____

    Air-conditioner cooling tower _____

    Carpet _____

    Hot-water heater _____

    Washers _____

    Dryers _____

    Pool surface _____

    Drapes _____

    Parking lot surface _____

• Did you have any trouble moving your furniture in? _____ S O T P R H N B

• Do all your locks work OK? _____ S O T P R H N B

• Are you related to any tenant in this building? _____ S O T P R H N B

_____

If so, examine those leases with a microscope.

• Are there any PCBs or asbestos in the building? _____ S O T P R H N B

_____

• Have you sold any other real estate? _____ S O T P R H N B

_____

SOTPRHNB • If so, please give me the name, address, and phone number of the last three persons or entities to whom you sold properties, and the addresses of the properties you sold. _____

_____

_____

_____

_____

_____

> The purpose of the previous two questions is to enable you to do a sort of credit check of the seller. Whenever you enter into an agreement to buy or sell real estate, you are, in effect, making an <u>unsecured</u> extension of credit to the other party. That's because if they fail to perform as agreed, it will cost you. It will cost you in wasted time and money spent and in opportunities missed. If you are doing an exchange, it could cost you the taxes which would be due if the seller screwed up your exchange.
>
> It is not prudent to extend credit without checking out the person to whom you are extending that credit. Explain that to the seller if he balks at answering these questions about other people to whom he has sold property. If he still balks, you may want to try to find out what other properties he's sold from the public records. But refusal to give such references is a danger sign which should make you especially wary of continuing to deal with this seller.

Additional interview notes:

PART SEVEN:
PREDICTING INCOME AND EXPENSES

22

Rental Comps

Fair-market-rental value

The seller and tenants will tell you what the rents are. As long as you ask **both** of them, you'll get the truth. The seller alone will often give you "projected" rather than actual rents.

But even if you have accurate information on what the rents currently are, you still need to know what the fair-market-rental value of the units is. They could be rented for too little. Or, in rare instances, for too much. The latter occurs when the seller fills the place with this relatives or others who will lie to you.

To get the fair-market-rental value, you have to find out what comparable units are renting for. To make sure they're comparable, you need to find out the following about them:

• Location _____

• Number of bedrooms?_____

• Square footage?_____

• Number of bathrooms? _____

• Central air-conditioning? _____

• Different rent for different floors? _____

_____

_____

> **This is always the case in high rises; sometimes in garden apartments.**

• Who pays the utilities: The owner or the tenant?
   Electric _____
   Gas _____
   Water _____
   Trash collection _____

• Do you have any of the following amenities:
   Swimming pool? _____
   Washer/Dryer in the apartment? _____
   Fireplace? _____
   Microwave oven? _____
   Cable TV? _____
   Frost-free refrigerator? _____
   Garbage disposer? _____
   Garbage compactor? _____
   Other? _____

_____

• Are the apartments furnished? (which ones? what's included?) _____

_____

_____

_____

• Are there any discounts, specials, or rent concessions? _____

_____

_____

• Do you have a health club? _____

• Number of parking spots per unit? _____

• Do you have covered parking? _____

• Do any of the units have a view? _____

• Are pets allowed? _____

• Do you have a 24-hour doorman? _____

• What security deposit do you require? _____

• What minimum lease term is required? _____

• Do the units have a balcony, patio, or yard? _____

• Do you provide drapes? _____

• Other considerations? (school district, etc.) _____

_____

_____

_____

_____

23

Income

Constructing an accurate income and expense statement

As the name implies, income property should produce an income. Rental property should produce rent. The most important skill an investor can possess is the ability to examine a building and accurately forecast its net operating income. This is not as difficult as it might seem for a beginner if he just uses a check list like this one.

Sellers and real estate brokers generally provide prospective purchasers with projected income and expense statements as a part of their marketing effort. **Ignore** these statements. These are known in the business as "liar's statements" because of the exaggerated figures they almost always contain. In fact, I took two courses given by subsidiaries of the National Association of Realtors® during which the instructors used the phrase "liar's statements" in telling ways.

The first course was Commercial-Investment 101, sponsored by the Commercial-Investment Division of the Realtors® National Marketing Institute, and was aimed at commercial real estate brokers. During that course, the instructors referred to income and expense statements prepared by sellers as "liar's statements" and directed the seminar attendees to reconstruct the income and expense statement in order to produce an accurate one.

Then I attended Property Management 101 sponsored by the Institute of Real Estate Management and aimed at property managers. They used the phrase "liar's statement" too. But when they used it, they were referring to statements prepared by real estate brokers. And they, too, said the course attendees would have to reconstruct brokers' statements so as to produce accurate ones.

They're both right.

No matter how much confidence you have in the owner or real estate agent, the income and expense statement is too important for you to rely on anyone else's version. It is virtually impossible for anyone but you to predict your expenses because so many of them will vary according to the way you manage the property. Some owners spend more money on upkeep than others. Some try to maintain 100% occupancy while others are willing to accept vacancies in order to get top rents.

Constructing an accurate income and expense statement is a **three-step process**. First, you must identify all the income and expense items that apply to the property. Then, you must verify the items which can be verified. Finally, you must estimate the things that vary according to the way you manage the property.

Income

Apartment or house rent is not the only type of income. Consider whether any of the other items on this list are or could be produced by this building, and also be alert to income types not listed here:

• Garage rent _____

_____

• Storage space rent _____

_____

> **At the apartment building I currently own, I rent three storage rooms, one of which is a sloped-ceiling closet under a stairway.**

• Laundry income _____

_____

• Furniture sales _____

_____

> **This is not a permanent source of income. But I've found it to be significant at the beginning of some of my investments. Many buildings have furniture left by tenants, furniture in apartments which have been rented as furnished, and appliances which are working but which**

> **the new owner wants to replace for marketing reasons. I have made money selling all of the above.**

• Other vending machine income _____

_____

• Swim club income _____

_____

• Rent on stores or offices _____

_____

• Interest on the building's bank accounts_____

_____

> **This interest would include both the interest on the security deposits (to the extent that state law allows you to keep it) and the interest on the building's checking account.**

• Security deposit forfeits _____

_____

> **This averages about 2% of the gross rental income of an apartment building. That's a lot of money. About the same as laundry income. Some would protest that forfeited security deposits are too small to include as income. But those same investors would almost invariably say that laundry income should be included.**
>
> **True, the forfeited deposits generally reimburse you for damages and lost rent. But you will no doubt include those expenses and lost rent in the expense and vacancy loss portions of your operating statement. So leaving out the forfeits gives an inaccurately low net operating income result.**

Additional notes on income:

24

Expenses

The first thing about expenses is make sure you don't overlook any. With this check list, you shouldn't.

• Fees

Accountant's fees _____

Attorney's fees _____

Government inspection fees _____

Property management fees _____

• Insurance

Boiler insurance_____

Fidelity bond insurance _____

Fire and casualty insurance _____

Flood insurance _____

Liability insurance _____

Pool insurance _____

Workers' compensation_____

Earthquake insurance _____

• Maintenance

Air-conditioning service contracts _____

Cleaning apartments upon turnover _____

Drape cleaning_____

Elevator service contracts _____

> **Count on having an elevator service contract whether the present owner has one or not.**

Extermination contracts_____

Heating system service contracts _____

Lawn maintenance_____

Painting apartment upon turnover _____

Painting apartments for long-term tenants _____

Pool service contracts _____

Repairs_____

Shampooing rugs upon turnover _____

Snow removal _____

• Payroll

FICA (social security tax) _____

FUTA (federal unemployment tax)_____

Leasing agent payroll _____

Maintenance payroll _____

State disability tax _____

State unemployment tax _____

Property taxes (include personal property taxes) _____

_____

• **Reserves** for:

Appliance replacement _____

Carpet replacement _____

Drapes or blinds replacement _____

Common area interior painting _____

Exterior painting _____

Furniture replacement _____

Resurfacing pool _____

Repointing brickwork _____

Roof replacement _____

Air-conditioner compressor replacement _____

Air-conditioner cooling tower replacement _____

Air-conditioner condenser replacement _____

Boiler replacement _____

Hot-water heater replacement _____

• **Utilities**

Electricity _____

Gas _____

Oil _____

Rubbish removal _____

Sewer _____

Telephone _____

Water _____

Vacancy losses _____

_____

Your vacancy rate will be a function of the rent you charge. If the present owner is enjoying a 100% occupancy rate and you plan to charge similar rents, there is no point in adding a 5% vacancy rate into

your calculation. If, on the other hand, you plan to raise rents substantially, you should include a vacancy estimate.

• **Miscellaneous**

Advertising (newspaper,) _____

_____

Sign rental _____

_____

When the building is not located on a high traffic street, owners often obtain permission from the owner of a property on a strategic corner to erect a sign that will direct prospective tenants to the property. These signs can be extremely important to your marketing effort, and the monthly rental fee paid to the landowner is an unavoidable expense that can be easily overlooked.

Apartment owners association dues _____

Some associations assess their members a flat dollar amount for each apartment. Be sure to include this incremental cost in your annual expenses.

Credit investigating service _____
Interest on security deposits _____

Many states require that all or part of this interest be paid to tenants. Such legislation is quite popular and will probably be passed in every state eventually.

Postage_____
Printing of forms, brochures, leases, etc. _____

_____

Supplies _____

Petty cash_____

Travel to and from the building if it's not near your home _____
_____

Subscription to local paper if not where you live _____

• **Other** _____

_____

_____

_____

_____

Additional notes on expenses:

25

Verify and Estimate

Once you've identified all the building's expenses, you need to either verify or accurately estimate them. Some expenses can be verified by speaking with the appropriate supplier or government agency. Don't hesitate to do so. Call or visit the municipal government and ask about or research the following:

• What is the total property assessment _____

• Assessment for land? _____

• Improvements? _____

• Will the property be reassessed upon sale? _____

• If not, when is the next reassessment scheduled? _____

• What is the current tax rate? _____

• Any indications of next year's rate? _____

• Are there any municipal improvements pending? _____

_____

_____

_____

• Is the municipal government considering any rent control legislation? _____

_____

_____

_____

In addition to knowing what the current property tax assessment is, you need to know what it's going to be next year. Because property taxes are generally your largest operating expense.

On November 30, 1983, I bought an apartment building for $835,000. It was reassessed effective January 1, 1984 at $1,002,505; up from the $500,000 which I had verified when I bought the place. That is, they doubled my assessment...which more than doubled my tax bill because the rate went up during the same period.

Obviously, $1,002,505 is too high an assessment for a property which was purchased 33 days earlier for $835,000. And I would have had good grounds for a tax appeal. But I didn't find out about the increased assessment until the end of 1984. My mortgage lender sent me a letter saying I owed them $6,573.66 to cover an escrow shortage. I said, "There must be some mistake."

The only mistake was my not checking on the new assessment sooner. By the time I found out about it, it was too late to file an appeal. I filed an appeal for 1985 and succeeded in getting the assessment reduced to $718,728.

In addition to verifying what the property tax assessment currently is on the building you are considering, you should also figure out what it ought to be. It may be lower than it should be. That's fine for as long as it lasts. But you should not base your purchase price on net operating income figures which are significantly higher than they would be if the property were properly assessed.

Base your offer on what the property tax assessment should be, not what it is. If the seller points to the abnormally low property tax assessment as evidence that you should up your bid, offer to give him a second mortgage which is contingent on the property tax bill staying

> below normal. For example, suppose the assessment were such that the current property tax bill was $5,000. But that comparable properties had tax bills of $9,000. You could agree to pay the seller annual payments equal to $9,000 minus the actual property tax bill for the year.

Utilities

Speak with the municipal water and sewage departments and other utilities (energy, rubbish removal, and so forth), and ask if they will give you figures for your prospective property for the past three years. They may insist on written permission from the current owner. If so, get it. If the current owner will not agree, find another building.

Also, find out any information you can about future rate increases.

• **Water** _____

• **Sewage** _____

• **Energy** _____

• **Rubbish** removal _____

• **Other** _____

_____

_____

> If the building or the domestic hot water is heated by oil, call the fuel dealer and find out <u>how many gallons</u> of oil were consumed in the last three years. Also ask about he <u>condition</u> of the heating system or hot water heater.
>
> If <u>pest control, elevator, or other service contracts</u> are in effect, call the contractors and ask about the condition of the building and the cost of their services.
>
> On such items as <u>insurance</u> and <u>service contracts</u> (which you plan to have but are not used by the current owner), call your agent or supplier to ask for a quote.
>
> Whenever you call about <u>consumables</u>, be sure that you receive information in the units of consumption: gallons of water, cubic feet of gas,

and so forth...since dollar figures quickly become outdated by inflation. To project your dollar expenses, multiply your anticipated cost per unit by the average number of units (gallons, cubic feet, kilowatt hours, etc.) consumed.

Many novice investors are surprised by the suggestion that they call the seller's creditors for information about that person's bills. They expect that the suppliers will be outraged by the request and indignantly hang up. Although this sometimes occurs, most suppliers will politely provide the information requested. Government agencies are usually required to make this information public, as are private utilities which are strictly regulated and must make their records available to the public. In come cases, utilities will request the owner's written permission to release the information you've asked for. Fuel oil dealers know that they will lose the old owner's business when the building is sold, and they see you as a potential customer.

So you need not demand the owner's tax return nor do you have to trick suppliers into releasing confidential information. Simply say that you are considering purchasing the property and need to verify the expenses.

Rents

The most important number on the income statement is the rental income. You should verify rental income in several ways. Ask the owner to show you leases, question the tenants about rents, and ask the tenants again by **letter** after you have signed the agreement but before you've reached a settlement.

The letter should state that the property has been sold and should include the main features of each lease:

• Rent amount _____

• Apartment number _____

• Names of occupants _____

• Security deposit amount _____

• Move-in date, lease term _____

• Special privileges (if any, or a statement that there are none) _____

_____

_____

• List of items, such as appliances, included in the rent _____

_____

_____

The letter should also state that, if any of the information is incorrect, the tenant should contact the buyer immediately.

Even if your have already seen the leases, follow this up with your letters; sellers frequently forge leases to inflate the value of their buildings.

Because there are many ways to disguise the true rent roll, your investigation should always include an appraisal of the fair market rental value of the apartments...based not on documents but on your observation of the apartments and your knowledge of the local market.

Estimation

Try to estimate pool, laundry, and other income in a similar way to your estimation of rental income. Speak with other building owners and laundry operators to determine how much of each type of income you can expect to make on the property you're investigating. If you provide a laundry concessionaire with the average size of the families in the building, he can usually give you an estimate of the revenue you can expect per apartment.

Payroll

Payroll is a very difficult item to estimate because it varies so widely. Some owners believe it is important not to skimp on the payroll, and they pay a high salary to their managers. Other owners pay far less, believing that this expense should be tightly budgeted. Since payroll is generally a large percentage of your total expense, it is important that you make as accurate an estimate as possible.

You can obtain a payroll estimate from the **Institute of Real Estate Management**'s *Income/Expense Analysis: Conventional Apartments*. This annual publication reports average operating statements for apartment buildings all over the country. The information is organized by region, city, property type, building age, and so forth. You can obtain a copy of this publication by writing to the Institute of Real Estate Management, 430 N. Michigan Avenue, Chicago, IL 60611.

If you are an experienced property owner, you should examine your own books to determine how much you've been spending on payroll. Confer with the other members of your local apartment owners association for their thoughts on compensation.

Also, there are many apartment associations, real estate brokerage companies, and real estate research companies which also produce statistical studies of local apartment income and expenses.

My book, *How to Manage Residential Property for Maximum Cash Flow and Resale Value* has a thorough chapter on "How much to pay your resident manager."

Replacement reserves

You must also estimate the remaining life of each part of the building that may need to be replaced and budget financial reserves to cover replacement costs. For example, let's assume that your binocular inspection of the roof reveals poor condition. You ask a roofer to inspect it, and he estimates it will last about five more years and quotes a replacement cost of $7,500. This $7,500 divided by five years is $1,500 per year, an "expense" which you must add to the income statement. By the time you replace the roof, its cost will undoubtedly be higher, but you probably don't have to worry about inflation here because your use of the money over the next five years should generate a return which at least keeps up with inflation.

Additional notes:

PART EIGHT:
<u>THE PURCHASE</u>

26

Negotiation

A check list alone can't make you a skilled negotiator, but it can help you become a **better** one by forcing you to map out your strategy in the calm before the storm and by helping you prepare thoroughly.

Once you have determined the price and terms you want, you should also decide upon your initial offer as well as the worst price and terms you are willing to accept. To determine your initial price and terms, think like a chess player who is plotting strategy for a match. Work backward from your target prices, through the most probable negotiating pattern, to an appropriate opening offer. You must be able to put yourself in the seller's shoes, and this requires that you find out as much as possible.

• How much did he pay for the property? _____

> You can usually find the owner's purchase price by checking the old deed in the county records. If the price you want to pay is close to his purchase price, he may resist because he will lose money after paying the selling commission. In this situation, you may want to offer the owner a higher, face-saving price, but be sure to demand excellent terms.

• What is his mortgage balance? _____

> From the mortgage balance, you will be able to compute the amount of money the owner will have after settlement. The seller is certain to calculate this number every time you change your offer, and if you want to know how your offers look to him, you should be prepared to do the same.

• Are there any other liens? _____

_____

> Most attorneys and buyers have a kneejerk reaction to all liens: pay them off at closing. Why would you want to do that? Liens are assumable. They are nonrecourse. You don't have to pay points or any other charge. They are interest only...no principal payments required. They generally carry only a low statutory rate of interest. And if the lienholder forgets about them, there may be a statutory expiration date.
>
> In view of the fact that liens are pretty good deals as loans go, why not just buy subject to them and give the seller that much less cash at closing?
>
> Of course, in many cases, the lienholder can do the opposite of forgetting about the lien. He can not only remember it. He can execute it. That is, get the sheriff to seize and auction off the property. Check with a local attorney to ascertain how likely that is.
>
> If you need new financing, some title companies will let you post a bond or deposit of, typically, 150% of the amount of the lien. Then they will remove the title policy exception for that lien. That makes the new mortgage, in effect, the first lien even though a title search would indicate that the new lender is junior to the lien. As long as the title company removes the exception from the lender's title insurance policy, the lender doesn't care if the lien is recorded senior to them and is still there.

• What does the seller plan to do with the proceeds of the sale? _____

_____

_____

_____

Taking back a second mortgage may offer an attractive alternative.

• What style did the seller use in previous negotiations? _____

_____

_____

_____

> The county's registry of deeds is a good source of the names of people with whom the seller has negotiated. Of course, you should also just ask him. Search for his name in both the "Grantor" and "Grantee" books, make note of the other parties, then try to contact them. As well as providing insights into the seller's negotiating style, a previous owner of your prospective purchase can tell you a great deal about the building's strengths and weaknesses. The mortgage books may reveal whether the seller has taken back a mortgage in the past and the terms to which he agreed.

• Think about the seller's tax situation - tax bracket and deadlines _____

_____

_____

_____

> If you ask subtle questions and note his employment and lifestyle, you can probably make an educated guess of the seller's income level. Of course, selling a property may change his bracket during the year of the sale. Try to calculate the amount of depreciation he's currently getting on the property and the portion of his mortgage payment that is nondeductible amortization. Tax laws are full of deadlines, and these can be powerful motivators.

• Make a list, in order of priority, of "throw-away" items - negotiating points that you
  will fight over initially, then concede as if they were very important to you:

_____

_____

_____

• Now write down the **initial** terms and price you'll offer, your **target** price and terms, and the **worst** price and terms you'll accept:

Initial offering price and terms _____

_____

_____

_____

Target price and terms _____

_____

_____

_____

Worst price and terms _____

_____

_____

_____

_____

> **This record will bolster you against the emotional storms that usually accompany such important negotiations.**

Additional negotiation notes:

27

What to Include in Your Purchase Agreement

The purchase agreement (also known as "purchase-and-sale agreement" or "deposit receipt" or "agreement of sale") is the most important document in the acquisition of a parcel of real estate and must be treated with great care. The following check list is included to aid you and your attorney and to be a basis for your discussions with him. It is **not** intended to be a substitute for an attorney.

Don't overlook your attorney's ability as a **negotiator**. If the real estate agent in the transaction is not a skilled negotiator or is unsympathetic to your cause, and your attorney is, ask your attorney to take part in the negotiations. Keep in mind, however, that attorneys, unlike real estate agents, charge by the hour. Keep the attorneys fees under control by authorizing one or two hours at a time. Don't give the attorney a blank check to take as much time as necessary. Attorneys who are given such blank checks tend to make very certain that your interests are very well looked after...**too** well looked after.

A purchase agreement has three essential elements:

• Names of the parties.
• Description of the property.
• Price and other terms of the sale.

Names of the parties

Not as simple as it sounds. Beware of dealing with sellers who sign as **corporations** or **partnerships**. And beware of the phrase "or assigns" or something similar after the name of the seller. The big problems at this point are making sure you're dealing with someone or some entity you can sue for specific performance in the event the seller fails to go through with the deal.

Also, you need to make sure the guy who signs the purchase agreement has the **authority** to do so. That is, he has the authority to sign for the entity which owns the property. And that entity really does own the property. It's important to know who you're dealing with.

Signing a purchase agreement is like loaning someone money. Because if the guy at the other end turns out to be a rat, it's going to cost you. Just like when you loan money to a guy who turns out to be a rat. Only with purchase agreements, the money you lose is called forfeited fees...for title searches, mortgage applications, etc...instead of a bad debt.

Description of the property

That means a legal description, not just the street address. **Read** the legal description. Check it against the other documents which contain it like the seller's deed, the mortgage, the title report, etc. If it's stated in metes and bounds, get a protractor, compass, and pencil and draw it on a piece of graph paper to make sure it's what you expect it to be. A company called AGT (404-924-9692) advertises an IBM compatible program called Deed-Chek for $99. It purportedly takes metes and bounds as its input and turns them into a survey-like map along with computing area and so forth.

You say legal descriptions make your eyes glaze over? Too bad. But you still have to read it. Or you may be paying for a property which is **less** than you think... or **different** than you think. Either would be a disaster. It has happened.

As most people know, the smallest details can be decisive in legal matters. For this reason, documents in real estate necessarily contain meticulous legal descriptions and seemingly endless details. Insist on such accuracy and detail in the legal papers governing your acquisition.

Title search

• Title insurance_____

_____   _____

> Specify title insurance company and policy. If you are doing an <u>exchange</u> spread over more than one town, it pays to use the same title company in each location. Specify <u>who pays</u> for the title insurance... usually set by local custom.
>
> Before any real estate purchase, you must make sure that the seller has the legal right to sell the property. This may sound ridiculous, but the danger that you may obtain an unclear title is real. For example, suppose that the sellers are a man and his second wife. If the man's

divorce from his first wife was granted by an authority not recognized by the state, the first wife may still retain part ownership of the property. If that is the case, a deed without her signature is not legally binding. Title insurance agents can give you dozens of similar examples.

ALWAYS HAVE A TITLE SEARCH MADE WHEN YOU BUY PROPERTY. Title insurance from a reputable company provides protection up to the face value of the policy. Your attorney may want to perform the search himself, as is common in Massachusetts, or he may want to have a title insurance company do it.

Clauses to consider

In addition to including the names of the parties, a description of the property, and the consideration and other terms of sale, ask your attorney to consider the following clauses:

• Disposition of existing mortgages _____

_____

_____

Are you going to pay off, assume or buy subject to the existing mortgages?

• Disposition of other existing liens _____

_____

_____

• Mortgage-contingency clause _____

_____

_____

If you need a new, institutional mortgage to buy the property, you need a mortgage-contingency clause. It says you don't have to go through with the deal if you can't get a mortgage. The seller will want a time limit. Make sure you get enough time.

This includes terms of any seller financing. How much is to be paid and when? And what are the details of the note and trustee deed or mortgage? You need to attach the <u>entire</u> mortgage (or trust deed) and note which will be used in the seller financing to the purchase agreement. If you only cite a few details in the purchase agreement, you may discover that you disagree strongly over the various mortgage clauses and find you don't have a deal.

• Date and location of settlement _____

_____

_____

• Termite certification _____

_____

_____

Spell out your right to inspect the property for termites and to get out of the deal if the seller fails to treat any infestation and/or repair any damage.

• Nature of title _____

_____

_____

"Good and marketable title" or "insurable title" are the least you should settle for.

• Type of deed and method of holding title _____

_____

_____

You want a general warranty or special warranty or grant or quit-claim deed, in that order of preference.

• Earnest money deposit _____

_____

> **How much and who holds it? If allowed by state law, state that the holder of the deposit is the seller's agent.**

• Prohibition against the seller entering into new, adverse leases _____

_____

_____

> **Seller may not enter into new, adverse leases prior to closing. That's to prevent him from leasing an apartment to his brother for 50 years at a below market rent after he shows you all the leases.**

• Proration of expenses, taxes, rents, interest on mortgages to be taken over and

security deposits _____

_____

_____

> **The income and expenses must be prorated as of closing day. If the building will have a <u>positive cash flow</u> for the month you buy it, you should try to get the seller to agree that <u>you</u> will be the owner <u>on closing day</u> for the purpose of the prorating calculation. If the building will have <u>negative</u> cash flow on closing day, you should get the seller to agree that <u>he</u> will be the owner on closing day for purposes of the prorating calculation.**
>
> **On a building with a $25,000 a year positive cash flow, each day is worth $25,000 ÷ 365 $68.49. If that was the only thing you learned from this $19.95 book, it has paid for itself.**

• Transfer of security deposits _____

_____

_____

• All personal property which is included in tenants' rent is to be included in the sale

(furniture, refrigerators, throw rugs, etc.) _____

_____

_____

• Inspection contingency _____

_____

_____

> **If you plan to inspect the property, or have others inspect it, after signing the purchase agreement, a smart seller will limit the time period. Make sure you get enough time.**

• Inspection of leases _____

_____

_____

> **Get the right to inspect all of the leases, including leases on vending machines, parking areas, and anything else. The seller will probably want a time limit.**

• Remedies if either party reneges _____

_____

_____

• Warranty that present use is legal to the best of seller's knowledge _____

_____

_____

> **Verify this after signing of the agreement by examining the local zoning ordinance.**

• Date possession is to be given _____

• Designation of who pays which fees, buyer or seller? _____

_____

_____

• Disclosure of whether either party holds a real estate license (such disclosure is usually required by state law) _____

_____

_____

• Permission to make a pre-closing inspection _____

_____

_____

• Warranty that the attached rent schedule and leases are accurate _____

_____

_____

• Seller must provide estoppel certificates signed by all tenants_____

_____

_____

> **One estoppel certificate in wide use asks for the identities of the landlord(s) and tenant(s), beginning and ending dates of the lease, address, rent, due date, how far into the future the rent has been paid, and security deposit amount. It also states that the lease is the whole agreement between the parties and that the landlord is not in default.**

• Warranty against default notices_____

_____

_____

> **Get the seller to warrant that he has not received any notice of default from the property's mortgage lenders or insurance companies.**

• Warranty against legal violations _____

_____

_____

> **Get the seller to warrant that he has received no notices that the building violates any building codes, fire regulations, etc.**

- Permission to show the property to contractors, insurance agents, buyers, or prospective tenants prior to closing (if appropriate) _____

  _____

  _____

- Warranty that there are no condemnation proceedings underway _____

  _____

  _____

- Permission to inspect all apartments if that has not been done prior to signing of the agreement of sale _____

  _____

  _____

- Keep building insured _____

  _____

  _____

> **Seller should promise to keep the building insured as presently insured through closing.**

- Survey _____

  _____

  _____

> **A surveyor should verify the boundaries. Thereby allowing you to remove the survey exception from the title insurance policy. Who pays is a matter of local custom or negotiation. You should have the right to get out of the deal if the survey turns up adverse information. The seller will probably want a deadline.**

• No side agreements _____

_____

_____

> **Clause stating that this is the entire agreement. There are no other agreements, verbal or written.**

Pre-closing inspection

The following items should be both in the purchase agreement and checked at the pre-closing inspection:

• Seller to provide inventory of personal property _____

_____

_____

> **This has tax implications. If you are <u>exchanging</u> into the property, you must exchange <u>real</u> property for <u>real</u> property and <u>personal</u> property for <u>personal</u> property. Also, one kind of personal property, coin-operated vending machines, is eligible for <u>first-year expensing</u>. All personal property is eligible for shorter cost recovery periods. Real property is not eligible for first-year expensing (except for new elevators and escalators) and its cost must be recovered over 27.5 years instead of five or seven.**
>
> **So unless it messes up your exchange, you want as high a value as possible placed on the personal property which comes with the building. That maximizes the present value of the new property's cost recovery deductions. For more information on the tax aspects of the deal, see my book *Aggressive Tax Avoidance for Real Estate Investors*.**

• Condition of the premises at the time the property changes hands (e.g., "broom clean") _____

_____

_____

> **Require seller to maintain the property as before until closing.**

•Warranty on equipment and systems _____

_____

_____

> **Get the seller to warrant that the plumbing, electrical, elevator, and heating, ventilating, and air-conditioning (HVAC) systems will be in working order and that the roof will be watertight as of closing.**

• Property damage will void the sale (at buyer's option) _____

_____

_____

• No new liens _____

_____

_____

> **Prohibit seller from adding new liens prior to closing.**

• Warranty that the plumbing, heating, and electrical systems are in working order
  at closing _____

_____   _____   _____

_____

• No bankruptcy_____

_____

_____

> **The seller warrants that he is not in the process of declaring, nor is he contemplating bankruptcy. If he declares bankruptcy within a year of your buying the property, it may be sucked back into the bankrupt estate as a fraudulent transfer in anticipation of bankruptcy.**

• Closing time and place _____

_____

_____

> Where (title company, attorney's office, or wherever) and when (date and time)? Many attorneys and lenders are pains in the neck about this. They insist closing be held in their office. When two parties in the same deal insist on different locations, you have a problem. Many of the people who are pains in the neck about this charge <u>extra</u> for attending closing somewhere else. If that's the case, try to hold the closing where the charge is <u>lowest</u>. If it's the <u>seller's</u> guy who insists on a more expensive location, make the seller agree to pay the resulting extra cost which you would otherwise incur.

• Assignment _____

_____

_____

> It would be nice if you had the right to assign (sell out your right in the purchase agreement). But a smart seller will want to control who's responsible for closing all the way through closing. Also, if there's seller financing involved, a smart seller will at least want to approve the credit of the assignee.

• Exchange clauses _____

_____

_____

> If you're doing an exchange into the house or apartment building in question, make sure your purchase agreement contains the clauses you need to make a valid exchange. For more information, see my book *Aggressive Tax Avoidance for Real Estate Investors*.

• Date of possession_____

_____

_____

It's not a good idea, but some times you get possession on a day <u>other</u> than closing. If it's <u>before</u> closing, your possession should be governed by a <u>lease</u>. If it's <u>after</u> closing, you must have the sale proceeds held in some sort of <u>escrow</u> so you're not left with neither your money nor the property.

• Mineral rights _____

_____

_____

If someone other than you has or will get the mineral rights, check the rights documents and state law. Mineral rights owners can legally do some pretty horrible things to the <u>surface</u> owner (that's you) in many cases. Make sure you know where you stand and...if the mineral rights will be owned by someone else...what the probability of exploitation and surface disturbance is.

• Foreigner _____

_____

_____

All sellers must give you an affidavit in which they state under penalty of perjury that they are not "foreign persons" (Canadians, for example) and give their United States taxpayer ID number (social security number for individuals) and address. If the seller is a foreign person, you, the buyer, must withhold 10% of the purchase price to make sure the seller pays his U.S. income taxes on the sale. Check the law on this if there's any doubt. Section 1445 of the Internal Revenue Code. <u>You could be liable</u> to IRS for that 10% if the seller <u>is</u> a foreign person and does <u>not</u> pay his tax.

• Notice or knowledge of toxic contamination _____

_____

_____

Seller must warrant that he has received no notice from any government or private entity or representative that the land or improvements

> contain any toxic substances. Nor does he have any reason to believe that the property has any toxic contamination.
>
> Try to get him to indemnify you against liability for any contamination which was on the property the day you acquire it. At the very least, the seller should indemnify you against any contamination which was caused by him or which he knew about or should have known about.

• Disclosures required by law _____

_____

_____

> The seller warrants that he has made all disclosures required by law to you.

Additional purchase agreement notes:

PART NINE: FINANCING

28

Financing

I'll discuss only **debt** financing in this book. Equity financing is a whole other subject. It would take a whole other book to cover it.

Avoiding default

Borrow the maximum you can safely repay. As long as the overall return you earn on the property exceeds the interest rate on the loan, you should borrow as much as you can repay.

Debt-coverage ratio

Safety regarding **monthly** payments is measured by your debt-coverage ratio. That's your net operating income divided by your mortgage payment. Net operating income is the rent and other income minus the operating expenses, but before debt service.

If your debt-coverage ratio is 1.00, you're operating at **breakeven**. That is, your monthly net operating income and your mortgage payment are equal (on average). If your debt-coverage ratio is **less** than 1.00, you have **negative before-tax cash flow**. If your debt-coverage ratio is **greater** than 1.00, you have **positive** before-tax cash flow.

You should not knowingly buy into a negative cash flow situation.

The amount by which your debt-coverage ratio exceeds 1.00 is your financial "shock absorber." It is also part of your return.

The higher the debt-coverage ratio, the better. Although, the seller has the opposite view to the extent that he wants to maximize his sale price and is not worried about your ability to make the payments on a seller mortgage. So it's hard to **get** a high debt-coverage ratio. As a general rule, try to get a debt-coverage ratio which would drop no lower than breakeven with however much vacancy loss is reasonably likely.

Home owner debt-coverage ratio

Home owners should use the same principle although the terminology is slightly different. A home owner does not look at the building's net operating income. Rather he looks at his family's own income. The net operating income of a family is its income from all sources less its non-housing expenses.

Balloon payments

You should not agree to any balloon payment which falls due sooner than **ten** years. I used to say seven years on balloons big enough to require refinancing of the property and no time limit on smaller balloons. I've since had to give an apartment building in Texas back to the guy who sold it to me. The main reason was that a seven-year balloon payment was coming up. The previous owner, who was a Californian and seemed not to fully understand the dynamics of a negative-equity, negative-cash-flow building, refused to renegotiate the non-recourse mortgage. So I said, "I quit."

I've noticed over the years that the older, more experienced, and presumably wiser investors all say ten years minimum on balloon payments. A study by the Seattle income property brokerage firm of Cain and Scott found that younger, less experienced investors agreed to shorter minimums. Here are their figures:

Time between origination and balloon payment

	1-5 years	6-9 year	10+ years
First-time investor	44%	31%	25%
Seasoned investor	18%	44%	38%

Inexperienced gurus also tend to be sanguine about short balloon payments. For example, Robert Allen, author of the book, *Nothing Down*, said five years. I used to say seven years. Jay Kaplan, former head acquisition guy at Consolidated Capital, said ten years.

Fixed versus adjustable rates

Adjustable-rate mortgages are insane. To agree to one without a cap is to sign a blank check. And you should only agree to an adjustable-rate mortgage **with** a cap if you can afford the worst case. Since the typical adjustable mortgage worst case interest rate is **higher** than the fixed rates available, it **never** makes sense to agree to a new adjustable-rate mortgage. (Assuming an already existing adjustable-rate mortgage which is at or near its cap **would** make sense. However, there has never been such a time since adjustable-rate mortgages were introduced in the early eighties.)

Getting a **new** adjustable-rate mortgage is financial Russian Roulette.

Assumability

Try to get a mortgage which is assumable by the guy you sell the building to. That's assumability with**out** any adjustment in interest rate. A fixed-rate mortgage protects your cash flow. But if it has a due-on-sale clause, that fixed-rate becomes "adjustable" on resale. That is, the buyer must get a **new** mortgage at **current** market rates. The higher those rates, the less you'll get for your building. So you want not only a fixed-rate but also assumability. Assumability protects your resale value to the extent of the proportion of the sale price represented by the existing mortgage.

FHA home mortgages originated before December 15, 1989 are assumable. FHA mortgages originated after that date are assumable only by owner occupants and then only if the FHA approves the new buyer's credit in advance.

FHA mortgages originated between December 1, 1986 and December 15, 1989 only require advance FHA credit approval if the resale takes place within **one** year of origination if the original borrower was an **owner occupant** and **two** years if the original borrower was an **investor**.

VA mortgages originated on or before February 29, 1988 are assumable if the buyer's credit is approved in advance by the VA.

Connections

Your connections may help you get a loan or better terms. Here's a list of possible connections who may be able to help you:

• **Family**: Parents, siblings, children, in-laws, etc. _____

_____

_____

• **Friends**: From each place you've lived, worked, attended school, armed forces, clubs, teams, etc. _____

_____

_____

• **Sellers**: Present and past_____

_____

_____

• **Tenants**: In present or past buildings_____

_____

_____

• **Members**: Of property owners, apartment owners, or other associations to which you belong_____

_____

_____

• **Advisers**: Attorney, accountant, broker, agent, etc. _____

_____

_____

• **Partners**: Business, real estate, golf, tennis _____

_____

_____

• **Dentist** _____

_____

• **Doctor** _____

_____

• **Professors**, teachers, adult-education instructors you've studied under _____

_____

_____

• **Employer** _____

_____

_____

• **Fellow students** in real estate seminars or adult education classes _____

_____

_____

How connections can help

The connections listed above may be able to help in one or more of the following ways:

• Providing equity money either as a general or limited partner _____

_____

- Co-signing or guaranteeing a loan _____

_____

- Lending you money _____

_____

- Purchasing assets you want to sell for more than you could get elsewhere

_____

_____

- Pressuring a lender with whom they have a business relationship _____

_____

- Transferring deposits or business to the lender with whom you are negotiating or threatening to withdraw them _____

_____

Seller financing and prepayment bonuses

When interest rates are high, sellers frequently take back mortgages at below-market interest rates. They do that in order to get the buyer to pay more for the property. In theory, it's OK to pay more in such circumstances. The proper premium would be the present value of the interest savings…discounted at the current market interest rate…over the life of the mortgage.

But note that last phrase: "life of the mortgage." If the seller gives you a ten-year mortgage at below-market interest rates, you can afford to pay more than the cash value of the building. Let's say the situation is this:

Mortgage amount:	$100,000
Market interest rate:	12%
Seller interest rate:	10%
Payment schedule:	Interest only with a ten-year balloon of principal
Monthly payments:	$833.33

Using a financial calculator, you can calculate the present value of that mortgage as follows:

Present value of monthly payments

n	=	120 months
i	=	1% per month
PMT	=	$833.33 per month

PV   = $58,084

Present value of balloon payment

n   =   120
i   =   1%
FV   = $100,000

PV   = $30,299

Adding the two present values, we get a total present value of $58,084 + $30,299 = $88,382. That's $100,000 - $88,383. = $11,617 less than the face amount of the mortgage so you could afford to pay that much **more** for the property as a result of the favorable interest rate on the seller mortgage.

But what if you pay the mortgage off **early**? That happens more often than you think. If the property goes up in value, you may want to sell or refinance. Interest rates could go down below 10% thereby making it sensible to refinance.

But if you pay the loan off early, you have to pay the **full $100,000**. Since the seller loan was only worth $11,617 if it lasted the full ten years, you screwed yourself by agreeing to overpay in return for the seller loan. For example, if you pay the loan off in just three years, the present value of the seller's mortgage rises to:

Present value of monthly payments

n   =   36 months
i   =   1%
PMT   = $833.33

PV   = $25,089

Present value of balloon payment

n   =   36
i   =   1%
FV   = $100,000

PV   = $69,892

For a total of $25,089 + $69,892 = $94,982. That's $94,982 - $88,383 = $6,599 more than you thought you were going to pay when you agreed, in effect, to pay an inflated price for the property in return for the ten-year loan.

In short, whenever you get a below-market interest rate seller mortgage, you should negotiate for a prepayment bonus. In other words, you should have the right to pay the mortgage off at a **discount** if you pay it off **early**. That discount should be spelled out in the loan documents. For example, it might say,

> *If this loan is paid off before its tenth anniversary, the amount required to pay it off will be the present value of the remaining payments when discounted at 12% per annum.*

Failure to get such a clause means that any prepayment will constitute an **unearned windfall** for the **seller** and a **hidden prepayment penalty** for **you**.

Right to substitute collateral

Institutions will generally not agree to it, but sellers who are taking back mortgages may agree to a substitution-of-collateral clause. As with subordination clauses, the courts will not enforce them if the seller/lender's interest is not protected to some reasonable degree. A fair substitution of collateral clause would allow you to substitute similar real property with at least equal value and equity. Or it may allow you to substitute bonds which will produce the same payment stream as the mortgage's scheduled payments.

The right to substitute bond collateral can be valuable if the market interest rate rises above the mortgage interest rate. You want to be able to substitute the lowest possible quality bond...because they are the cheapest for you to buy. For example, you might specify that you have the right to substitute bonds of at least a CCC rating by one of the major bond rating agencies.

When you decide to exercise your right to substitute collateral, you show up with your bonds and the seller/lender is required to release the property from the mortgage.

Other things you should check when shopping for a mortgage

• Amount _____

_____

_____

• Interest rate _____

_____

_____

• Term _____

_____

_____

• Payment pattern (balloons? self-amortizing? How much must you pay and when?)

_____

_____

_____

• Security instrument? (First mortgage, second mortgage, trust deed, land contract, etc). _____

_____

_____

• Loan fees:

Appraisal _____

Application fee _____

Assumption or transfer fee _____

Discount points _____

Lender's attorney fee_____

Fee for engineering report required by lender_____

Loan broker's commission _____

Mortgage insurance premium _____

Credit investigation fee _____

Recording fees_____

Tax service fee_____

• Truth-in-lending fee (This applies only to owner-occupied homes.)

_____

• Other fees paid to lender _____

_____

_____

> **Ask if the above fees are all the charges the lender will expect you to pay. Do this in writing so that you get a written answer. Do it early enough so that you can find another lender if there are unacceptable fees.**

• Fees paid to other than lender but due to loan _____

_____

_____

• Prepayment penalty (How much and under what circumstances is it due?)

_____

_____

_____

• Length of commitment period _____

_____

• Personal liability _____

_____

> **Will you be personally liable for all or part of the loan or will the property be the lender's sole security? See my book *How to Use Leverage to Maximize Your Real Estate Investment Return* for more information.**

• Impound accounts (For which expenses?) _____

_____

_____

_____

• Who makes payments on existing loans? _____

_____

_____

> **If a wraparound mortgage is used, the buyer typically makes payments to the _second_ lender or an escrow agent who, in turn, makes payments to the _first_ mortgage lender. This is _not_ a _requirement_ of a wraparound. Although most investors think it is. It's best for you to send the payments _directly_ to the first mortgagee; second best to let an escrow agent do it. Letting the seller/second mortgage lender do it is dangerous. He may pocket all the money instead of paying the first.**

• Will there be a vendor's lien in the deed? _____

_____

> **Don't ask this question. It might put an idea in the lender's mind that wasn't there before. But note it if one of the lenders you're considering says they want it.**

• Where are payments made? _____

_____

• Payment due date (Grace period?) _____

_____

• Late penalty_____

_____

> I've never paid a mortgage late penalty. So I'm not very interested in what the amount is. You shouldn't be either. But, all things being equal, the loan with the lowest late penalty is best.

• Define notice:

How mailed and to whom at what address? _____

_____

How much notice and time to cure _____

_____

> I used to think notice clauses were mere "boilerplate." No more. In 1988, I got into a dispute with a guy who took back a mortgage when he sold me an apartment building. During the dispute, this kind of "boilerplate" became important. You must get the right to a reasonable amount of notice in the event of default on the mortgage. And you must get reasonable amount of time to cure any defaults.

• Subordination clause _____

_____

_____

> This clause subordinates the mortgage to a future mortgage. Future subordination is very tricky and hard to write in a way that is legally enforceable.
>
> Institutional lenders will rarely agree to such a clause. But sellers often

will. However, if there is inadequate protection of the seller/lender's interest, the clause will probably **not** be enforceable in court.

Future subordination clauses are most likely to make sense for all concerned and the courts when the new loan will be used to finance value-increasing improvements to the property in question. The brief, broad subordination clauses which "creative finance" seminar gurus advocate are laughably unenforceable.

• Cross collateralization and cross default clauses _____

_____

_____

If you have more than one mortgage with the same lender, they may require cross-collateralization and cross-default clauses. Those clauses enable them to foreclose on each property so covered even if you default on just one. You should avoid agreeing to those clauses when you can.

• Sunset clauses _____

_____

_____

You should try to get as many sunset clauses as you can. They are **hard** to get from **institutional** lenders. But **sellers** will **often agree** to them. Sunset clauses terminate some security aspect of the mortgage after a certain period of time has passed or another criterion has been satisfied. For example, a sunset clause might say that you are required to have private mortgage insurance until your loan-to-value ratio drops below 80%.

• What does the lender require regarding:

Hazard insurance _____

_____

Title insurance _____

_____

Appraisal _____

_____

Survey _____

_____

Termite inspection and certification _____

_____

Flood insurance _____

_____

Assuming existing loans

If you plan to assume or buy subject to an existing loan, make sure your attorney checks the existing loan documents very carefully to be sure that assumption or buying subject to will not trigger an enforceable due-on-sale clause.

Also, do not assume that all existing loans with interest rates that are below current market interest rates should be preserved. In general, if the loan to value ratio of the existing loan is 30% or less, you should refinance no matter what the interest rate on the existing loan. That's because the existence of the first mortgage forces you to either make a huge down payment or obtain a second mortgage. Both are very expensive and thereby cancel out the benefits of the low interest rate on the existing loan.

Furthermore, existing loans which are many years old have high constants. That is, the annual payment total divided by the current loan balance is quite high...higher than the constant of a **new** mortgage even with its higher interest rate. In other words, old, low-interest-rate mortgages require higher monthly payments per thousand of loan than new, higher-interest-rate mortgages because the amortization payments on the old mortgages are so high.

Oddball mortgage types

Since the seventies, a lot of oddball mortgages have been offered...like shared appreciation mortgages, reverse annuity mortgages, graduated payment mortgages, etc.. I'll not discuss them in this book because I don't have room. Consult my book, *How to Use Leverage to Maximize your Real Estate Investment Return* for more information.

• Right of first refusal to buy mortgage_____

_____

_____

> **Try to get a right of first refusal to buy the mortgage. If the lender decides to sell it, typically at a discount, you get 90 days or some such to match the buyer's price. Equivalent to a prepayment discount.**

Additional notes on financing:

PART TEN:
THE CLOSING

29

Closing Preparation

Real estate brokerage, title, and mortgage companies typically use legal-size file folders which have check lists printed on their outside. Those check lists cover the many items which have to be taken care of to get a deal through closing. As a buyer, you need a similar check list.

Utilities

You need to have the utilities read their meters on closing day so you don't pay for the period before your ownership. You should also read the meters yourself during your pre-settlement inspection in case the utility doesn't make it on closing day.

• Electric _____

> Make sure **each** meter is read. Some buildings have just one meter. Others have different meters for each building, each apartment, common areas, etc.

• Gas _____

• Water _____

• Telephone _____

> **Tell the phone company your starting dates on the service if you are taking over an <u>existing</u> phone number at the property. They will also need authorization from the seller to transfer the use of that number to you. If you are getting one or more <u>new</u> phone lines, make arrangements with the phone company for installing them.**

• Cable TV _____

> **Tell the company your starting date if you have to pay for cable service either as a user or as a landlord.**

• Homeowners association _____

• Heating oil _____

> Heating oil is <u>delivered</u>, not metered. The standard prorating practice is to have the oil delivery man "stick the tank" on closing day. That is, he takes the cap off the top of the storage tank and puts a measuring stick in. He then reads the depth of oil in the tank, converts it to the number of gallons based on a chart for that size tank, and gives the seller a written estimate of the amount of oil in the tank and its current value. The written estimate is given to the title clerk at closing for proration calculations.
>
> You should check the depth yourself at your pre-closing inspection. You should also check the price as of closing day to make sure the oil dealer isn't quoting an inflated price as a favor to the outgoing owner.

• Trash _____

> **If there is a bill for monthly trash collection (there's not where municipalities collect it), tell the company your name and address and when you will become the owner.**

Property taxes

Tell the government entities which tax your new property **when** you will become the new owner and the mailing **address** to which you want the tax bills sent.

Renovation

If you plan to renovate the property immediately after closing, you'll need to get contractors into the property before closing.

Insurance

Call several insurance agents to get quotes on insuring the property and arranging for coverage to begin on closing day. This is extremely important. Properties have been known to burn down on closing day...often in fires set by spiteful former owners or employees of the property. Institutional lenders will not allow closing to proceed unless evidence of required insurance is provided by the buyer at closing.

Use the insurance check list in the "Expenses" chapter of this book...and the lender's requirements for insurance...as your check list when ordering insurance.

Some insurance companies need to inspect the property in order to quote on it.

Employees

If the building you are buying has or will have a resident manager, leasing agent, maintenance staff, etc., you need to take a number of steps before closing.

• Give termination notice to the previous employees if appropriate _____

_____

• Give eviction or termination of lease notice to the previous employees if appropriate

_____

• Place help-wanted ad for new employees if appropriate _____

_____

> **See my book, *How to Manage Residential Property for Maximum Cash Flow and Resale Value* for detailed information on how to recruit and compensate new employees.**

• Get employees to fill out IRS Form W-4 (Employee's Withholding Allowance Certificate) _____

_____

• Get employees to fill out and provide supporting documentation required by Immigration and Naturalization Service Form I-9 (Employee Eligibility Verification) _____

_____

• Get employees to sign employment agreements _____

_____

Subcontractors

• Heating/air-conditioning service contractor _____

_____

• Elevator service contractor _____

_____

• Exterminator _____

_____

• Laundry concessionaire (who is actually a **tenant** with a written lease) _____

_____

_____

• Gardener _____

_____

> **Outside subcontractors like the five listed above need to be informed of the change in ownership and/or terminated and replaced as appropriate.**

Miscellaneous

• Order new stationery if appropriate _____

_____

• Give forwarding order to post office if you are moving into the property in question

_____

• If you are moving into the property, send change of address to:

Periodicals you subscribe to _____

_____

Friends and relatives _____

_____

Credit card companies _____

_____

Other creditors _____

_____

State department of motor vehicles _____

Insurance companies _____

_____

Alumni associations _____

_____

Clubs _____

_____

Bank accounts you plan to keep _____

_____

• Register to vote in the new neighborhood _____

_____

• Register children in schools _____

_____

- Transfer medical and dental records _____

_____

_____

- Open new safe deposit box _____

- Open new bank accounts _____

_____

- Join local apartment owners or real estate investors associations _____

_____

- Start delivery of newspaper in new area _____

_____

> **Rental property owners who do not live near their building will probably want to subscribe to the newspaper serving the area where the building is located.**

Notice to tenants

Tenants need to be informed of the ownership change. The notice needs to be signed by the landlord named in their leases as well as by you. Unless they are so notified, they could send their rent to the **seller** and **refuse** to begin sending it to **you** unless they are provided incontrovertible proof of your right to it.

Estoppel certificate

The seller is generally required to provide the buyer with an estoppel certificate signed by each tenant. You must monitor whether these certificates are complete and delivered to you by the agreed-upon deadline.

Termite inspection

Order an inspection by a reputable termite company. Make sure they plan to give you some sort of guarantee. These days, many termite guys will charge you a fee to go out to the property, then give you a meaningless report which makes no guarantees.

Survey

Title insurance policies generally contain an exception for encroachments by adjoining property owners. You have to get a new survey in order for them to remove that survey exception. Buyers who chose not to do that have been hurt badly. I know of one instance in which the state widened a highway into the backyards of many homes. The state did not take the land from the home owners. The state had always owned it. But they weren't using it so the builder staked out the lots onto the state right of way. Home owners lost not only part of their yard...but, in some cases, garages and swimming pools. Those who had obtained surveys when they bought were compensated by their title insurance companies. But home owners who chose to save the survey fee, had to absorb the loss.

In general, you should order a survey which will enable the title insurer to remove the survey exception to their policy when you buy property.

Remove contingencies

Your purchase agreement generally contains contingencies like your ability to obtain a mortgage, satisfactory inspection reports, etc. Those contingencies must be complied with **in writing** by certain **deadlines** or the deal is dead. You need to order those inspections and apply for those mortgages in a timely fashion. You must send or deliver the written mortgage commitments and/or your letter lifting contingencies so that they arrive in a timely fashion.

If it appears that you **cannot** make one or more of those deadlines, you must obtain written amendments to the purchase agreement to extend those deadlines or else the purchase agreement may become unenforceable.

Additional notes on closing preparation:

30

Pre-Closing Inspection

You always make a pre-closing inspection. The reason is that the seller may not have complied with the purchase agreement in some way. He may have stripped the building of items which he was supposed to leave. He may have failed to clean part of the property which was supposed to be cleaned. A tenant you were counting on may have moved.

The time to find out about these things is **before** closing.

Before closing, you have tremendous power. You can refuse to sign the necessary papers if everything is not as you had bargained for. But that power drains almost totally out of you...instantaneously...as soon as they get your signature. So do **not** sign closing papers until the purchase agreement has been fully complied with.

Take with you to pre-closing inspection

• Purchase agreement and related addenda _____

• Inspection aid items listed in Chapter 10 _____

The inspection

The pre-closing inspection need not be anywhere near as thorough as the original inspection. You're looking for the following:

• Cleanliness _____

_____

_____

> I once was the agent on the sale of a house which was owned by an elderly woman. She was in a nursing home and it was clear she would never return home. The house was packed to the ceilings with junk and was filthy. The church which was handling her affairs promised in the purchase agreement to leave the property "broom clean."
>
> On closing day, I told the buyers it was time to make the pre-closing inspection. They didn't want to be bothered. I insisted. They still didn't want to be bothered. Although I had no reason to believe anything was wrong with the house, I did know that a pre-closing inspection was an absolute necessity. I told them I'd lay down on the floor and hold my breath until I turned blue if they didn't make that inspection. They didn't take that literally. But I had made my point. They made the inspection.
>
> The house was a disaster. True, it was far better than before. And the church volunteers no doubt deserved medals for the gargantuan labor they had performed. But the place was still a disaster.
>
> The wife said it was not clean enough and asked what they should do. I said they had to refuse to close until it was clean enough or withhold enough money from the seller/church at closing to cover paying someone else to finish the job.
>
> To the wife's horror, the husband said, "Nah, don't worry about it. We'll accept it as is." And they did.
>
> For weeks afterward, the wife called me to demand that the real estate company I worked for compensate her for the clean up. Her husband had assigned her the task. I told her the time to demand compensation was at closing and the people to demand it from were the church folks, not my company. And I reminded her that it was I who had insisted on the pre-closing inspection which gave them the opportunity to demand compensation at closing. Eventually, she quit calling.

• Systems in working order _____

_____

> Your purchase agreement should say the heating, air-conditioning, plumbing, electrical, and elevator systems are to be in working order at time of closing. Well, this is it, baby. Time of closing. Speak now or forever hold your peace. Test every system. Including the off-season climate control. That is, test the heat in August and the air-conditioning in January if possible. If you don't, you may be very sorry. You may later learn that the system does not work at all and must be completely replaced. Big bucks.

• No damage _____

_____

> Something may have happened to the building since you inspected it the first time. Vandalism, hit by truck, fire, you name it. Check to make sure any such damage has been repaired.

• Personal property _____

_____

> Compare what's there with the inventory of what you're buying. The seller may have substituted a broken down lawn mower for the one you saw. Or older lobby furniture. Or whatever.

• Oil inventory _____

_____

> If the building is heated by oil, you need an inventory of the fuel tank on closing day. You're typically required to buy that oil at closing from the seller. So you want to make sure you don't get charged for a <u>full 550</u>-gallon tank when the building only has a <u>half-empty 125</u>-gallon tank. Note the gauge reading if there is one. Use a stick if there isn't. A rough measurement is good enough.

• Read the meters:

Electric _____

Gas _____

Water _____

> **The utilities will also be doing that on closing day. Your readings are to compare with the utility readings to make sure no mistake has been made.**

Additional notes on pre-closing inspection:

31

Closing

Take to closing

• Purchase agreement and addenda _____

_____

• Filled-out settlement statement _____

_____

You will get a settlement statement from the title or escrow clerk who handles your purchase. But I want you to also fill one out yourself <u>in advance</u>. Then you compare the one the title company fills out and asks you to sign to the one you filled out. Ask for an explanation of any discrepancies.

The reason for this is closing is neither the time nor the place to be reading and analyzing complicated settlement statements. You need to do that reading and analysis in private...at your leisure. If you wait

> until closing, there's a very high probability that you'll leave money on the table by overlooking an omission or not spotting an error.
>
> The settlement statement you do should <u>not</u> be a "rough cut." It should be the real thing. As accurate and thorough as you can make it. I accomplish that by calling the title or escrow clerk several weeks in advance. Then when I've completed mine, I send it to the title or escrow clerk to ask if it contains any errors or omissions. Often, I've noticed that the clerks use <u>my</u> preliminary settlement sheet as their guide in preparing the real thing. Good. Better mine that the seller's.

• Your attorney, if any _____
_____

> He or she need not be there in person. I typically call my attorney the day before closing to find out where he will be during closing. And I take the phone number where he can be reached to closing.
>
> My attorney being absent has never caused a problem. Matter of fact, I've had more problems caused by attorney <u>presence</u> than by their absence. I've spent many an hour staring at the ceiling while other people's attorneys argued over legal trivia at closing.

• Portable financial calculator _____

• Pencil (They don't run out of ink.) _____

• Pad of paper _____

• Mortgage commitment and related file, if any _____

• Mortgage or trust deed and note _____

> For the same reason you don't look at the settlement statement for the first time at closing, you don't look at the mortgage or trust deed you're going to sign for the first time at closing. Get copies in advance...blank copies if that's all that's available. And read them at a quiet time and place. Better yet, <u>type</u> the entire documents into a word processor. That will cause you to spot things you overlook on even the most careful reading.

You may want to make a photocopy of the mortgage and note you study in advance on a transparency. (Most ordinary photocopiers can do this.) Then at closing, you lay that transparency <u>over</u> the mortgage or note they want you to sign. If they're the same, the letters will line up. If not, any differences will show up immediately.

You think that's overdoing it? There have been cases where sellers substituted different, printed forms for the ones the buyer thought he would be signing. Sometimes drastically different due to the addition of one little word like "or." And court cases have said, "Tough" to chagrined buyers who signed documents different from what they thought they were signing. "Read before you sign," is standard business practice say the courts. You ignore that advice at your peril.

I'll remind you of how much money's at stake here. Hundreds of thousands of dollars. Millions of dollars in the typical apartment building deal. Tens of thousands or hundreds of thousands of dollars can turn on an "or" or an "and" in the loan documents. Would you put it past <u>all</u> the sellers and lenders in the world to spend $100 on typesetting and printing to slip an adverse change past you?

• Cashier's check _____

For the amount you'll need and then some. Seller's and title companies often will not accept personal checks.

• Regular check book _____

Sometimes, title companies and sellers will accept a personal check... especially for small amounts. It doesn't hurt to take it just in case.

• Fire insurance policy or binder _____

• Notarized documents _____

_____

If you need the signatures of someone who cannot attend closing, have them sign them in front of a notary and bring those documents.

- Power of attorney _____

> If you can't get the signature of absent parties on pertinent documents in advance in front of a notary, you need a notarized power of attorney from those individuals. It's good to get that even if you think they have already signed all the documents they need to sign. Furthermore, make sure the <u>exact wording</u> of the power of attorney is approved in advance by the attorneys for the lender and seller. My last closing got all screwed up because my buyers brought a <u>revocable</u> power of attorney from their absent partner. The lender's attorneys insisted on an <u>irrevocable</u> power of attorney. We had to have the guy sign a faxed copy of the mortgage and note in front of a representative of the lender in the absent partner's city.

- Cheering section _____

> In some parts of the country, like California, there is no formal closing ceremony. Rather each party signs papers separately, in advance. Where there is a formal closing in a conference room, as in New Jersey and Texas, it's a good idea to bring a cheering section.
>
> The most logical people would be partners, attorney, accountant, spouse, your grown children. Theoretically, they should be superfluous. But in reality, there are often disputes at closing. The other party's cheering section will put heavy pressure on you to resolve it <u>his</u> way. So you need to bring your <u>own</u> cheering section as a counterweight. Of course, if you're the only one with a cheering section, so much the better.

- Oil price _____

> Check the current price of number two heating oil before you go to closing. Otherwise, the seller may try to overcharge you the way rental car places charge you inflated prices for gas if the rental car tank is less than full when you return it.

At closing, you do three things:

1. Make sure everything is in order.
2. Sign papers.
3. Get the signatures of others and such things as keys.

Do **not** rely on the escrow people to protect you. They make mistakes. Sometimes **big** ones. You are the only one who will protect your interests. Here are some of the most common discrepancies you should look for:

• Income and expense proration _____

_____

_____

> **Make sure the right party got the income and expenses for closing day itself. Also, watch out for rents paid prior to closing which are entirely for a period after closing. They should <u>not</u> be prorated. As when a tenant pays his rent for April on March 10th and closing is on March 20th.**

• Interest proration _____

_____

_____

> **The lender tells the title or escrow company how much to get from you. Often, they assume that the check paying off the old loan will arrive a week after closing. So they tack seven more days interest onto the amount you owe. On a $500,000 13% mortgage, that'd be $1,246.58! In a pig's eye!**
>
> **Tell the escrow company to <u>wire</u> the money to the lender...at your expense if necessary...and to <u>not</u> charge you for any interest beyond closing day. Indeed, on a large loan, you should check the exact wording of the loan being paid off to see if you owe interest for the day they receive the money.**
>
> **Also carefully check the calculation of interest you are required to pay on a <u>new</u> mortgage. One day's interest is a lot in income-property deals.**

• Wrong party charged _____

_____

> The purchase agreement may say that the seller pays for title insurance. But the escrow company may charge the you, the buyer by mistake.

• Charge omitted _____

_____

_____

> I used to fill out settlement statements in advance... but only <u>my</u> portion of the statement. <u>Not</u> the other guy's side. <u>Now</u> I fill out <u>both</u> sides. That's because of a deal I did in 1978.
>
> My buyer agreed to pay the attorney's fees for the preparation of the assumption documents. I handed the title clerk my attorney's bill for the buyer to pay. The buyer's attorney said, "I'd like to see that." Then he never gave it back to the title clerk and it was forgotten...until I got a dunning notice from the attorney. I called the buyer. He told me to drop dead.
>
> Fortunately, I had used the same title company for the entire five-way exchange. And they mistakenly paid me too much at the Texas end. I gave them back the excess...after I deducted the attorney's fee. In other words, the title company ended up paying the attorney's fee because I handed them the bill and they failed to notice that the buyer's attorney pocketed it. So no harm done. But you can't expect such luck. Look at <u>both</u> sides of the settlement statement and make sure the other guy is paying everything he agreed to pay.

• Double charge _____

_____

> Sometimes, you pay for items <u>before</u> closing. Like hazard insurance, attorney's fees, and mortgage fees. Make sure you don't pay <u>again</u> at closing. Also, make sure they aren't charging <u>both</u> the buyer and the seller for something that only one or the other is required to pay.
>
> Finally, make sure you don't double pay by having something deducted from your side of the settlement sheet then paying again in the form of a check for the same amount. I did that in that same 1978 deal. The rent security deposits on one building I was selling were deducted from my proceeds and credited to the buyer. Plus, I brought a check for the amount in the security deposit account. Fortunately, I had

> maintained good relations with the buyer. He spotted the error and returned the check at closing (after I had left)!

• Security deposits _____

_____

_____

> Make sure any security deposits paid by tenants who have not moved in yet are credited to you. If the tenant has not moved in yet, he will not appear on the rent schedule. The security deposit credit is usually a column on the current rent schedule. Since the space will be vacant on the rent schedule, it will look normal for no security deposit to be listed for that space. But if the tenant paid the security deposit before closing and signed a lease saying so, you're liable for it when he moves out. That happened to me also. But the seller agreed and sent me a check.

Things to get at closing

• Deed _____

• Signatures correct? _____

• Your name and the names of any co-owners correctly stated? _____

• Property description correct? (read every single word and compare to correct description). _____

• Right kind of deed? (general warranty, grant, etc.) _____

• Correct method of holding title? (tenants-in-common, joint tenants, etc.)_____

• Bill of sale for the personal property that comes with the building _____

• Copy of mortgage or trust deed and note _____

• Settlement statement _____

• All leases _____

• Assignment of all leases to you _____

• Assignment of building name, if any, to you _____

• Assignment of building's phone number to you _____

• All keys _____

• Termite certification with satisfactory wording _____

• Title insurance policy _____

• Hazard and liability insurance policy _____

• Survey _____

• Mortgage payment instructions_____

• Building permits, if any _____

• Certificate of occupancy, if any _____

• Warranties and instructions on building equipment _____

• Tenant credit files for skip tracing, market research_____

• Sign permits _____

• Letter to tenants signed by seller saying building has been sold effective closing
   date and to whom they should pay rents in future_____

• Seller's name, future address, and phone number _____

_____

• Property manager's name, address, and phone number _____

_____

• Oil inventory (Basically, a receipt for the oil you bought from seller in oil-heated building. Needed for taxes.) _____

Additional notes on closing:

APPENDIX A
Seller Interview Questions

This appendix groups the questions you should ask the seller of the property you're interested in buying. For background information on these questions, refer to Chapter 21.

• From whom did you buy the property?_____

_____

• Why are you selling the property? _____

_____

• What do you plan to do with the sale proceeds?_____

_____

• Will this sale be part of an exchange? _____

• Have you had any roof leaks? _____

_____

_____

• Have you had any underground pipe leaks? _____

_____

• Have you had any underground tank leaks? _____

_____

• Have you had pests?
    Termites? _____
    Roaches? _____
    Mice? _____
    Rats? _____
    Any other vermin?_____

- Is the building exterminated regularly? _____

- Have you had any problems with the air-conditioning system? _____
  _____

- Have you had any crime in the neighborhood or in the building? _____
  _____

- Have you had any plumbing problems? _____

- How many (which) apartments, if any, have furniture rented from the owner of the
  building? _____

- Is there flooding in the basement or elsewhere on or near the property during or after
  heavy rains? _____

- Are there any tenants you wish were not here? _____
  _____
  _____

- Do you have any parking problems? _____
  _____

- Have you had any trash removal/dumpster problems? _____
  _____

- Have you had any snow removal/ice problems? _____

- Have you had any problems with elevator service? _____
  _____

- Have you had any smog in the area? _____
  _____

• Is there a noise problem in the building or in the neighborhood? _____
_____

• Have you had any problems with the janitorial service? _____
_____

• Are you satisfied with the performance of the manager? _____
_____
_____

• Do you have a waiting list? _____

• Which oil dealer do you use? (where applicable) _____
_____

• How many electric, gas, and water meters do you have? _____

• Have you appealed your property tax assessment? If so, what were the results?
_____
_____

• Do you allow pets? _____

• Have you had any problems with the heating system? _____
_____

• Have you had any problems with the electrical system? _____
_____

• Is there enough hot water? _____

• Is there adequate water pressure? _____

• How well has the heating system been maintained? _____
_____

- How well has the air-conditioning system been maintained? _____

  _____

- When were the following last replaced?

  Roof _____

  Boiler _____

  Air-conditioner compressor _____

  Air-conditioner cooling tower _____

  Carpet _____

  Hot-water heater _____

  Washers _____

  Dryers _____

  Pool surface _____

  Drapes _____

  Parking lot surface _____

- Do all your locks work OK? _____

- Are you related to any tenant in this building? _____

  _____

- Are there any PCBs or asbestos in the building? _____

  _____

- Have you sold any other real estate? _____

  _____

- If so, please give me the name, address, and phone number of the last three persons
  or entities to whom you sold properties, and the addresses of the properties you
  sold. _____

  _____

  _____

  _____

  _____

Additional seller interview notes:

APPENDIX B
Previous Owner Interview Questions

This appendix groups the questions you should ask the **previous** owner of the property you're interested in buying. For background information on these questions, refer to Chapter 21.

• Did you had any roof leaks? _____

_____

_____

• Did you had any underground pipe leaks? _____

_____

• Did you had any underground tank leaks? _____

_____

• Did you had pests?

  Termites? _____

  Roaches? _____

  Mice? _____

  Rats? _____

  Any other vermin? _____

• Was the building exterminated regularly? _____

• Did you had any problems with the air-conditioning system? _____

_____

• Did you had any crime in the neighborhood or in the building?

_____

• Was there flooding in the basement or elsewhere on or near the property during or

  after heavy rains? _____

• Did you had any plumbing problems? _____

• Were there any tenants you wished were not there? _____

_____

_____

• Did you have any parking problems? _____

_____

• Did you have any trash removal/dumpster problems? _____

_____

• Did you had any snow removal/ice problems? _____

• Did you have any problems with elevator service? _____

_____

• Did you have any smog in the area? _____

_____

• Was there a noise problem in the building or in the neighborhood? _____

_____

• Did you have any problems with the janitorial service? _____

_____

• Were you satisfied with the performance of the manager? _____

_____

_____

• Did you have any problems with the heating system? _____

_____

• Did you have any problems with the electrical system? _____

_____

• Was there enough hot water? _____

• Was there a problem with the water pressure? _____

• Why did you sell? _____

• When did you sell? _____

• What were the price and terms? _____

• What was your asking price? _____

• Do you remember the buyer's first offer? _____

• Were there any problems in the negotiations? _____

• Would you do business with him again? _____

• Were there any problems on closing day? _____

_____

• Would you be willing to own the property again? _____

    If not, why not? _____

_____

_____

• When were the following last replaced?

    Roof _____

    Boiler _____

    Air-conditioner compressor _____

    Air-conditioner cooling tower _____

    Carpet _____

    Hot-water heater _____

    Washers _____

    Dryers _____

Pool surface _____

Drapes _____

Parking lot surface _____

• Did all your locks work OK? _____

• Are there any PCBs or asbestos in the building? _____

_____

Additional previous owner interview notes:

APPENDIX C
Tenant Interview Questions

This appendix groups the questions you should ask tenants in the property you're interested in buying. For background information on these questions, refer to Chapter 21.

• Have you had any roof leaks? _____

_____

_____

Have you had pests?

    Termites? _____

    Roaches? _____

    Mice? _____

    Rats? _____

    Any other vermin? _____

• Is the building exterminated regularly? _____

• Have you had any problems with the air-conditioning system? _____

_____

• Have you had any crime in the neighborhood or in the building? _____

_____

• Have you had any plumbing problems? _____

• Is there flooding in the basement or elsewhere on or near the property during or after

    heavy rains? _____

• Are there any tenants you wish were not here? _____

_____

_____

• Do you have any parking problems? _____

_____

• Have you had any trash removal/dumpster problems? _____

_____

• Is the air-conditioning adequate? _____

• Are your appliances all in good working order?_____

• Have you had any drain stoppages? _____

• Do your intercom and remote door opener work properly? _____

• Have you had any snow removal/ice problems? _____

• Have you had any problems with elevator service? _____

_____

• Have you had any smog in the area? _____

_____

• Is there a noise problem in the building or in the neighborhood? _____

_____

• Have you had any problems with the janitorial service? _____

_____

• What rent do you pay? _____

• Did you receive, or are you going to receive, any rent concessions? _____

_____

• How much is your security deposit?_____

• Do you plan to renew your lease when it expires? _____

• Are you satisfied with the performance of the manager? _____

_____

_____

• Is the exterior lighting adequate? _____

• Are the laundry facilities adequate? _____

• Have you made any improvements to your apartment? _____

• Does your water ever have an odor or color? _____

• Do you rent the furniture in the apartment? _____

• Do any of your toilets run continuously? _____

• Do any of your faucets drip? _____

• Do the apartments' trash containers generally have enough room for your trash?

_____

• Are you satisfied with the policies which govern the swimming pool? _____

_____

• Do you know of any safety hazards on the property? _____

_____

• Are your door locks adequate? _____

• Are your window locks adequate? _____

• Have you had any problems with the heating system? _____

_____

• Have you had any problems with the electrical system? _____
_____

• Is there enough hot water? _____

• Is there adequate water pressure? _____

• Did you have any trouble moving your furniture in? _____

Additional tenant interview notes:

APPENDIX D
Property Manager Interview Questions

This appendix groups the questions you should ask the property manager of the property you're interested in buying. For background information on these questions, refer to Chapter 21.

• Have you had any roof leaks? _____

_____

_____

• Have you had any underground pipe leaks? _____

_____

• Have you had any underground tank leaks? _____

_____

• Have you had pests?

    Termites? _____

    Roaches? _____

    Mice? _____

    Rats? _____

    Any other vermin? _____

• Is the building exterminated regularly? _____

• Have you had any problems with the air-conditioning system? _____

_____

• Have you had any crime in the neighborhood or in the building? _____

_____

• How many (which) apartments, if any, have furniture rented from the owner of the building? _____

- Have you had any plumbing problems? _____

- Is there flooding in the basement or elsewhere on or near the property during or after heavy rains? _____

- Are there any tenants you wish were not here? _____
_____
_____

- Do you have any parking problems? _____
_____

- Have you had any trash removal/dumpster problems? _____
_____

- Have you had any snow removal/ice problems? _____

- Have you had any problems with elevator service? _____
_____

- Have you had any smog in the area? _____
_____

- Is there a noise problem in the building or in the neighborhood? _____
_____

- Have you had any problems with the janitorial service? _____
_____

- Do you have a waiting list?_____

- Which oil dealer do you use? (where applicable)_____
_____

- Do you allow pets? _____

• Have you appealed your property tax assessment? If so, what were the results?

_____

_____

• Have you had any problems with the heating system? _____

_____

• Have you had any problems with the electrical system? _____

_____

• Is there enough hot water? _____

• Is there adequate water pressure? _____

• How well has the heating system been maintained? _____

_____

• How well has the air-conditioning system been maintained? _____

_____

• Do all your locks work OK? _____

• Are there any PCBs or asbestos in the building? _____

_____

Additional property manager interview notes:

APPENDIX E
Resident Manager Interview Questions

This appendix groups the questions you should ask the resident manager of the property you're interested in buying. For background information on these questions, refer to Chapter 21.

- Have you had any roof leaks? _____

    _____

    _____

- Have you had any underground pipe leaks? _____

    _____

- Have you had any underground tank leaks? _____

    _____

- Have you had pests?

    Termites? _____

    Roaches? _____

    Mice? _____

    Rats? _____

    Any other vermin? _____

- Is the building exterminated regularly? _____

- Have you had any problems with the air-conditioning system? _____

    _____

- Have you had any crime in the neighborhood or in the building? _____

    _____

- Have you had any plumbing problems? _____

- How many (which) apartments, if any, have furniture rented from the owner of the building? _____

- Is there flooding in the basement or elsewhere on or near the property during or after heavy rains? _____

- Are there any tenants you wish were not here? _____

_____

_____

- Do you have any parking problems? _____

_____

- Have you had any trash removal/dumpster problems? _____

_____

- Is the air-conditioning adequate? _____

- Are your appliances all in good working order? _____

- Have you had any drain stoppages? _____

- Do your intercom and remote door opener work properly? _____

- Have you had any snow removal/ice problems? _____

- Have you had any problems with elevator service? _____

_____

- Have you had any smog in the area? _____

_____

- Is there a noise problem in the building or in the neighborhood? _____

_____

• Have you had any problems with the janitorial service? _____

_____

• What rent do you pay? _____

• Did you receive, or are you going to receive, any rent concessions? _____

_____

• How much is your security deposit? _____

• Do you plan to renew your lease when it expires? _____

• Is the exterior lighting adequate? _____

• Are the laundry facilities adequate? _____

• Have you made any improvements to your apartment? _____

• Does your water ever have an odor or color? _____

• Do you rent the furniture in the apartment? _____

• Do any of your toilets run continuously? _____

• Do any of your faucets drip? _____

• Do the apartments' trash containers generally have enough room for your trash?

_____

• Are you satisfied with the policies which govern the swimming pool? _____

_____

• Do you know of any safety hazards on the property? _____

_____

• Are your door locks adequate? _____

• Are your window locks adequate? _____

• Do you have a waiting list? _____

• Which oil dealer do you use? (where applicable) _____
_____

• How many electric, gas, and water meters do you have? _____

• Do you allow pets? _____

• Have you had any problems with the heating system? _____
_____

• Have you had any problems with the electrical system? _____
_____

• Is there enough hot water? _____

• Is there adequate water pressure? _____

• How well has the heating system been maintained? _____
_____

• How well has the air-conditioning system been maintained? _____
_____

• When were the following last replaced?
    Roof _____
    Boiler _____
    Air-conditioner compressor _____
    Air-conditioner cooling tower _____

Carpet _____

Hot-water heater _____

Washers _____

Dryers _____

Pool surface _____

Drapes _____

Parking lot surface _____

• Did you have any trouble moving your furniture in? _____

• Are you related to any tenant in this building? _____
_____

• Are there any PCBs or asbestos in the building? _____
_____

Additional resident manager interview notes:

APPENDIX F
HVAC Contractor Interview Questions

This appendix groups the questions you should ask the heating, ventilation, and air-conditioning contractor, if any, of the property you're interested in buying. For background information on these questions, refer to Chapter 21.

• Have you had any underground pipe leaks? _____

_____

• Have you had any underground tank leaks? _____

_____

• Have you had any problems with the air-conditioning system? _____

_____

• Have you had any plumbing problems? _____

• Is there flooding in the basement or elsewhere on or near the property during or after heavy rains? _____

• Have you had any problems with the heating system? _____

_____

• Is there enough hot water? _____

• Is there adequate water pressure? _____

• How well has the heating system been maintained? _____

_____

• How well has the air-conditioning system been maintained? _____

_____

• Are there any PCBs or asbestos in the building? _____

_____

Additional HVAC contractor interview notes:

APPENDIX G
Neighbor Interview Questions

This appendix groups the questions you should ask neighbors of the property you're interested in buying. For background information on these questions, refer to Chapter 21.

• Have you had any crime in the neighborhood or in the building?

_____

• Is there flooding in the basement or elsewhere on or near the property during or after heavy rains? _____

• Are there any tenants you wish were not here? _____

_____

_____

• Do you have any parking problems? _____

_____

• Have you had any trash removal/dumpster problems? _____

_____

• Have you had any snow removal/ice problems? _____

• Have you had any smog in the area? _____

_____

• Is there a noise problem in the building or in the neighborhood? _____

_____

Additional neighbor interview notes:

APPENDIX H
Other Buyer Interview Questions

This appendix groups the questions you should ask other buyers who have bought from this seller of the property you're interested in buying. For background information on these questions, refer to Chapter 21.

• Were there any problems in the negotiations? _____

• Were there problems with the property which you feel the seller should have told you about beforehand? _____

_____

• Have you had any problems with the previous owner since you bought it?

_____

• Would you do business with him again? _____

• Were there any problems on closing day? _____

_____

Additional other buyer interview notes:

APPENDIX I
Business Trip Check Lists

Here's a check list to use when packing to go on or return from a business trip. You will almost certainly need to add items which are unique to you. But this list covers most things.

Business Supplies
- note pad
- mechanical pencil
- business cards
- calculator
- computer
- dictation recorder
- addresses and phone numbers of contacts in the destination city
- Day-Timer calendar
- check book
- telephone answering machine remote beeper
-
-
-

Miscellaneous
- before leaving, pay bills which will fall due during trip
- books to read on plane
- plane ticket
- wallet
- cash for tips and other items
- travelers cheques
- luggage keys
- street map of distant city
- camera
- prescription medicine you are taking
-
-
-

Clothes
- underwear for each day
- socks/hose for each day
- shoes for each event
- pants for each event
- shirts for each event
- ties/scarves
- suits
- belt
- sport coats
- rain coat
- warm coat if cold weather
- gloves if cold weather
- hat
- handkerchiefs
- pajamas
- bathing suit
- athletic clothing and equipment if you plan to work out during trip
- sunglasses
- spare glasses
-
-
-

Toiletries
- razor
- shampoo (now often provided by hotels)
- toothbrush
- dental floss
- toothpaste
- nail clippers
- tweezers
- birth control devices or medicines
- deodorant
- comb/brush
- hair dryer
- contacts cleaner
- make-up/lotions
-
-
-

Business trip expense check list

For tax purposes, you need to keep detailed records of your business expenses. Here's a check list to help you do that. If you have a computer and spreadsheet software, you should create a spreadsheet in this format and type over the old entries each time you go on a business trip.

Date	Meals	Miles	Park	Tips	Tolls	Trans	Misc
MEALS							
Breakfast							
Lunch							
Dinner							
Other refreshments							
TRANSPORTATION							
Home to airport							
Airport parking							
Bridge toll							
Highway toll							
Air fare							
Airport to hotel							
Rental car							
TIPS							
Baggage tip/home airport							
Bag tip/destination airport							
Baggage tip/curb to lobby							
Baggage tip/lobby to room							
MISCELLANEOUS							
Hotel							
Laundry							

APPENDIX J
Pertinent References

Aggressive Tax Avoidance for Real Estate Investors. John T. Reed. Annual. Reed Publishing.

Cain and Scott Apartment Investment Study. Cain and Scott, Inc. Annual. Seattle, WA.

Finding and Buying Your Place in the Country. Les Scher. Collier Books.

How I Turned $1,000 Into $5,000,000 in Real Estate in my Spare Time. William Nickerson. Simon & Schuster.

How to Buy a House in California. Warner, Serkes & Devine. Nolo Press.

How to Manage Residential Property for Maximum Cash Flow and Resale Value. John T. Reed. Reed Publishing.

Income/Expense Analysis: Conventional Apartments. Annual. Institute of Real Estate Management. Chicago, IL.

Minimum Property Standards for Multifamily Housing. U.S. Department of Housing and Urban Development. Washington, DC.

Peace of Mind in Earthquake Country. Peter Yanev. Chronicle Books.

Real Estate Investor's Monthly. John T. Reed. Newsletter. Reed Publishing.

Residential Foundations: Design, Behavior and Repair. Robert Wade Brown. Van Nostrand Reinhold Company.

INDEX

Your Opinion of this Book is Important to Me

Please send me your comments on this book. I'm interested in both compliments and constructive ciriticism. Your compliments provide guidance on what you want. And, with your permission, I'd like to use your favorable comments to sell future editions of the book. Constructive criticism also helps make the book's next edition better.

Evaluation of *Residential Property Acquisition Handbook*

Circle one: Excellent   Good   Satisfactory   Unsatisfactory

Circle one: Too Advanced   About Right   Too Basic

What part did you like best? _____

_____

What part did you like least? _____

_____

How can I improve the book? _____

_____

My promotional material includes brief comments by people who have read the book and their name, (company name in some cases), city, state, and occupation. I would appreciate any remarks you could give me for that purpose:

_____

_____

_____

Name _____ Occupation _____

Address _____

City _____ State _____ Zip _____

Feel free to leave blanks if you prefer not to answer all of these questions. I would appreciate receiving your evaluation even if you only fill out one line.

How long have you been a real estate investor? _____

What is the total value of your investment real estate? _____

What types of property do you own? _____

If your comments will not fit on this sheet, feel free to write them on the back of additional sheets. Please send your evaluation to:

John T. Reed
342 Bryan Drive
Danville, CA 94526

John T. Reed's Order Form

	Unit Price	Total

Newsletter

		Unit Price	Total
_____ one-year subscriptions to John T. Reed's Real Estate Investor's Monthly (12 monthly issues)		$121.00	$_____
_____ back issues (Please see catalog for list. <u>Minimum order is 3.</u>) 1 to 11 back issues		$ 8.50 ea.	$_____
	12 or more back issues	$ 8.00 ea.	$_____
	All back issues starting Feb. '86	$ 7.50 ea.	$_____

Special report

	Unit Price	Total
_____ copies of Single-Family Lease Options (48 pages)	$ 29.95	$_____
_____ copies of Distressed Real Estate Times: Offensive and Defensive Strategy	$ 29.95	$_____

Books

	Unit Price	Total
_____ copies of Aggressive Tax Avoidance for Real Estate Investors — 10th Edition	$ 23.95	$_____
_____ copies of How to Increase the Value of Real Estate	$ 19.95	$_____
_____ copies of How to Manage Residential Property for Maximum Cash Flow and Resale Value	$ 21.95	$_____
_____ copies of Office Building Acquisition Handbook (loose leaf)	$ 39.95	$_____
_____ copies of Real Estate Investor's Monthly on Real Estate Investment Strategy	$ 39.95	$_____
_____ copies of Residential Property Acquisition Handbook	$ 19.95	$_____

Cassettes (Two 60-minute cassettes in a binder)

	Unit Price	Total
_____ copies of High Leverage Real Estate Financing	$ 29.95	$_____
_____ copies of How to Buy Real Estate for at Least 20% Below Market Value, Vol. I	$ 29.95	$_____
_____ copies of How to Buy Real Estate for at Least 20% Below Market Value, Vol. II	$ 29.95	$_____
_____ copies of How to Find Deals That Make Sense in Today's Market	$ 29.95	$_____
_____ copies of How to Manage Residential Property for Maximum Cash Flow and Resale Value	$ 29.95	$_____
_____ copies of How to Save Tens of Thousands of Tax Dollars by Exchanging	$ 29.95	$_____
_____ copies of Lease Options, Single-Family Residences	$ 29.95	$_____

Software

	Unit Price	Total
_____ copies of Landlording™ On Disk software by Leigh Robinson **IMPORTANT—CHECK ONE**: ☐ Macintosh ☐ IBM 5 1/4 ☐ IBM 3 1/2"	$ 39.95	$_____
	Subtotal	$_____

Discount 5% for two or more items totaling over $100 $_____

California residents: add your area's **sales tax** (except on newsletter subscription) $_____

Shipping: $4.00 for first item $ 4.00

$2.00 for **EACH** additional item $_____

For a **Rush Order,** add $5 more to the shipping costs) $_____

(Including shipping, a subscription is $125 for one year and

there is **one** shipping charge for any number of back issues.)   **Total** $_____

Satisfaction guaranteed
or your money back

Method of Payment: _____ Check enclosed payable to John T. Reed   _____ Visa   _____ MasterCard   _____ Discover

Credit card # _____ Exp. Date _____ Signature _____

Ship to: Name _____

Street Address* _____

City _____ State _____ Zip _____ Telephone _____

* UPS cannot deliver to P.O. boxes. Please allow 2-3 weeks for processing and delivery.

Please mail your order to: John T. Reed, P.O. Box 27311, Concord, CA 94527

These prices are effective May 1, 1991 and are subject to change. Source Code: 03

For faster service, ☎ phone toll-free:

800-635-5425

John T. Reed's Order Form

	Unit Price	Total

Newsletter

		Unit Price	Total
_____ one-year subscriptions to John T. Reed's Real Estate Investor's Monthly (12 monthly issues)		$121.00	$_____
_____ back issues (Please see catalog for list. <u>Minimum order is 3.</u>) 1 to 11 back issues		$ 8.50 ea.	$_____
12 or more back issues		$ 8.00 ea.	$_____
All back issues starting Feb. '86	$	7.50 ea.	$_____

Special report

	Unit Price	Total
_____ copies of Single-Family Lease Options (48 pages)	$ 29.95	$_____
_____ copies of Distressed Real Estate Times: Offensive and Defensive Strategy	$ 29.95	$_____

Books

	Unit Price	Total
_____ copies of Aggressive Tax Avoidance for Real Estate Investors — 10th Edition	$ 23.95	$_____
_____ copies of How to Increase the Value of Real Estate	$ 19.95	$_____
_____ copies of How to Manage Residential Property for Maximum Cash Flow and Resale Value	$ 21.95	$_____
_____ copies of Office Building Acquisition Handbook (loose leaf)	$ 39.95	$_____
_____ copies of Real Estate Investor's Monthly on Real Estate Investment Strategy	$ 39.95	$_____
_____ copies of Residential Property Acquisition Handbook	$ 19.95	$_____

Cassettes   (Two 60-minute cassettes in a binder)

	Unit Price	Total
_____ copies of High Leverage Real Estate Financing	$ 29.95	$_____
_____ copies of How to Buy Real Estate for at Least 20% Below Market Value, Vol. I	$ 29.95	$_____
_____ copies of How to Buy Real Estate for at Least 20% Below Market Value, Vol. II	$ 29.95	$_____
_____ copies of How to Find Deals That Make Sense in Today's Market	$ 29.95	$_____
_____ copies of How to Manage Residential Property for Maximum Cash Flow and Resale Value	$ 29.95	$_____
_____ copies of How to Save Tens of Thousands of Tax Dollars by Exchanging	$ 29.95	$_____
_____ copies of Lease Options, Single-Family Residences	$ 29.95	$_____

Software

_____ copies of Landlording™ On Disk software by Leigh Robinson

IMPORTANT—CHECK ONE: ☐ Macintosh   ☐ IBM 5 1/4   ☐ IBM 3 1/2" $ 39.95 $_____

	Subtotal	$_____

Discount 5% for two or more items totaling over $100 $_____

California residents: add your area's **sales tax** (except on newsletter subscription) $_____

Shipping: $4.00 for first item $ 4.00

$2.00 for **EACH** additional item $_____

For a **Rush Order,** add $5 more to the shipping costs) $_____

(Including shipping, a subscription is $125 for one year and

there is **one** shipping charge for any number of back issues.)   **Total** $_____

Satisfaction guaranteed
or your money back

Method of Payment: _____ Check enclosed payable to John T. Reed   _____ Visa   _____ MasterCard   _____ Discover

Credit card # _____   Exp. Date _____   Signature _____

Ship to: Name _____

Street Address* _____

City _____   State _____   Zip _____   Telephone _____

* UPS cannot deliver to P.O. boxes. Please allow 2-3 weeks for processing and delivery.

Please mail your order to: John T. Reed, P.O. Box 27311, Concord, CA 94527

These prices are effective May 1, 1991 and are subject to change. Source Code: 03

**For faster service, ☎
phone toll-free:**

800-635-5425